In a tribute to this living, buzzing, always changing, yet never changing metropolis
we call home, Orange is proud to be associated with *Bombay Gothic*.

the future's bright, the future's Orange

BOMBAY GOTHIC

BOMBAY GOTHIC

CHRISTOPHER W LONDON

IBH

INDIA BOOK HOUSE PVT LTD

CONTENTS

PREFACE   8

INTRODUCTION   10

A 'MODERN' STYLE FOR BOMBAY   13
   Afghan Memorial Church (1847-58)   16
   Sir Jamsetjee Jeejeebhoy School of Art (1874-78)   20
   Governor Frere's Plan (1862-67)   25
   Watson's Hotel (1868-71)   31

HIGH GOTHIC DREAM   35
   Frere Town   36
      The Secretariat (1867-74)   38
      University Buildings (1868-80)   40
      High Court (1871-78)   52
      Public Works Department Office (1869-72)   54
      General Post Office (1869-72)   56
      David Sassoon Library & Reading Room (1867-70)   58
   Beyond the Fort Precinct   60
      CJ Building for Elphinstone College, Byculla (1866-71)   60
      Crawford Market (1866-71)   62
      Emerson's Churches (1866-72)   67
      David Sassoon Building for Elphinstone High School (1872-79)   72
      Chief Presidency Magistrate's Court (1884-89)   74

CLIMAX OF BOMBAY GOTHIC   77
  Victoria Terminus (1878-88)   79
  Royal Alfred Sailors' Home (1872-76)   96
  Battle of Styles   98
    Bombay Municipal Corporation Building (1889-93)   99
  In Quest of the 'Correct' Style   106
    Mulji Jetha Fountain (1892-93)   106
    Bombay, Baroda & Central Indian Railway Offices (1894-99)   107
    Army & Navy Cooperative Society Store (1897)   112
    Chartered Bank of India, Australia & China (1899-1902)   113
    British India Steam Navigation Building (1900-03)   114
    Royal Bombay Yacht Club Residential Chambers (1896-98)   115

CONCLUSION   119

APPENDIX   127
  Central Events   128
  Bombay's Architectural Development   129
  Architectural Styles   131
  Architects & Artists   138
SELECT BIBLIOGRAPHY   143
GLOSSARY   144
STREET NAMES/ILLUSTRATIONS   148
CREDITS   149
INDEX   150

Preface

One of Mumbai's most arresting qualities is its abundance of European-style buildings, with each architectural era amply represented. This book considers the history of selected exceptional Victorian buildings in the city. Mumbai's neo-Gothic buildings represent 'high fashion' of the 19th century. With deep verandas and resplendent arcades, these Gothic buildings possess a novel look within the worldwide output of this style. Their finely carved Indian stone and exceptional tile and interior woodwork details set new standards for design excellence in the subcontinent. The buildings' site-specific 'handmade' appearance is rare for their time, showcasing as it does the various communities of India, and its animals, plant life, historic and distinguished local citizens in sculptural detail. This should be a source of delight to the patient observer, even today.

The use of Gothic in Mumbai denotes the city's interaction with the architectural fashions of the world stage. The internationalism of the style in the 19th century serves as a testament to the power of trade, shared printed design resources, and the discovery that architects – as teachers and practitioners – as well as component building parts could be 'exported' successfully to India and elsewhere. Ottawa in Canada and Melbourne, Australia, are other cities that are included in this Victorian Gothic architectural heritage. In the 19th century, the world shared common perceptions of fashion and there was a significant European influence upon world affairs. In Mumbai, the confluence of these varied forces created an Indian neo-Gothic style of rare charm.

Mumbai has so many extraordinary neo-Gothic buildings because Governor Frere, in 1862, tore down the walls of Bombay's fort. A convinced Gothic enthusiast, he thereby freed up large tracts of land for building, devised a master plan for the city, and implemented his vision during his five-year tenure. He left Bombay before most of the buildings he planned were complete, but the stamp he left on the city is indelible in an area now sometimes referred to as 'Frere Town'.

University Convocation Hall; multifoil stained glass window showing the coat of arms of England.

Bombay Gothic may often appear more elaborate and awkward than the High Gothic structures of Britain. This could be ascribed to a more restricted supply of available designers at Bombay than those readily on hand in Europe. However, because of the Indian craftsman's preference for elaboration, it is also richer in detail, which surely adds interest to the buildings. Each one was approached as a singular project, and only a small proportion of mass-produced terracotta motifs were used for their decoration; the rest was specially devised for the commission. Buildings on the *maidans* were isolated within their own garden setting and were constructed of varied polychromatic combinations of stone. The planners of Bombay were fortunate in that they had open land to work with. Furthermore, adjustments made to the Gothic architecture of Bombay, adaptations for climate and the sunlight, for instance, enabled architects to explore subtle shifts in approaches to construction, which arose partly from necessity in India. Perhaps Bombay Gothic is the more extraordinary for its adaptations to site, climate and materials drawn from the design sources of Europe. However, this book should help the reader to engage with and understand what is available in Mumbai, in order to come to a fair assessment of this question.

Introduction

Ownership of Bombay's islands transferred from Portugal to Britain in 1661, when Charles II married Catherine of Braganza, a Portuguese princess. Bombay grew as an urban centre under the direction of the British who brought their aesthetic values with them from 'home'. In the 18th and early 19th centuries, they experimented with the neo-Classical style of architecture, but then, suddenly, the city charted a new course that reflected contemporary European fashions. The study of medieval structures had resulted in distinct architectural trends in northern Europe and Britain. To develop a more national style, perhaps, building forms began to be based increasingly upon vernacular types rather than upon ancient Greek and Roman precepts. In a rapidly industrializing century, this style looked back to the markedly pre-industrial era when 'barbaric' Goths overran Europe to end the Classical age. Gothic architecture of the medieval ages became high fashion, admired for its human scale and the manual construction techniques its appearance evoked.

Gothic architecture uses the pointed rib vault as its constructional technique. The Classical style uses the round arch. The sources for Gothic architecture relate closely to carpentry and wooden timber constructions. Gothic style buildings express their purpose quite directly on their exterior form. So, verticality, articulated by externally perceptible staircases, large open halls, functional areas, or visible methods of managing load, is observable on the outside of these buildings. This legibility of function is a hallmark of the Gothic. Further significant characteristics are the desire to be functional and practical as opposed to elegant, and the embrace of angular, pointed, bulging, or jutting forms allied with irregular floor plans. Neo-Gothic actively rejects the symmetrical and balanced compositions so admired by the classicist. The Classical aesthetic strives to achieve restfulness with an orderly monochromatic presence, whereas the Gothic style is expressive, disturbing and disjointed with lively coloured surfaces. Flying

The Mint (1829), a balanced neo-Classical composition; note central pediment and columns.

buttresses, lancet windows and stained glass are noteworthy features of such architecture, and its buildings are often embellished with carved and narrative elements. Indeed, the very name of the style, Gothic, is derived from the Goths who invaded Europe from the north, ending the Classical era, and through this style these barbarian peoples remain associated with both a political and an architectural history.

Neo-Gothic architecture first became popular in Britain in the 1750s and 1760s. However, the first neo-Gothic buildings were not historic sources for Bombay's architecture; they merely encouraged further study of medieval buildings. Then, in the 19th century, many distinguished architects undertook protracted study of Gothic buildings. The architects AWN Pugin, George Edmund Street, William Burges, George Gilbert Scott and Samuel Sanders Teulon are but a few of a large group of Gothic Revivalists who designed churches and other buildings based upon their extensive research into medieval forms. They made drawings, authored publications, photographed and restored medieval buildings with great seriousness. Architectural and religious societies also formed to direct and spread the popularity of the neo-Gothic in the 19th century. These groups and individual architects offered explanatory printed advice on how to construct such buildings and argued for their 'correctness'.

As the 19th century progressed, its architects justified the use of numerous past architectural styles as appropriate for any given building. The practice led to an eclecticism that established a great range of decorative options. Whether Bombay is the victim of this Victorian tendency to accumulate stylistic precedents, or merely the happy recipient of such eclectic trends, is for the reader to decide.

A 'MODERN' STYLE FOR BOMBAY

THE FIRST GOTHIC BUILDINGS

A RANGE OF NEO-GOTHIC INFLUENCES can be discerned in Bombay's buildings. The 'muscular' Gothic style, a 19th century style based on the ideal of truth to nature, expresses the building's function boldly on its exterior. It also displays a preference for heavy and massive forms. Venetian Gothic popularized the use of arcaded façades, with details counterpointed in stone of various colours, a lively style much appreciated in India. French Gothic architecture in Bombay came to mean a loose combination, with English Gothic, of French architectural forms such as the *flèche*. A delicate, floriated, and elaborate sculptural scheme for windows, vaults, capitals and buttresses usually accompanies the French Gothic style. Early English Gothic architecture of the 12th and 13th century employed the characteristic pointed arch, but was more austere in appearance and cheaper to build than the Decorated style that followed – the style of London's Westminster Abbey.

The Decorated style was promoted by the Victorian avant-garde who were influenced by the Ecclesiological Society. It prescribed this late 13th century and early 14th century style as the only suitable one for church architecture. Later styles were considered decadent, while the earlier,

Muscular Gothic details (griffins and exaggerated heavy forms) on dome of Elphinstone High School (left). French Gothic window tracery and fine carved-stone surround on High Court (right).

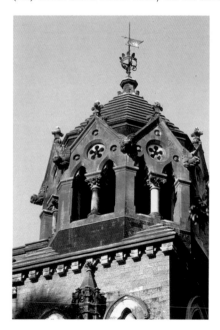

Watercolour of Sir Jamsetjee Jeejeebhoy Hospital, Byculla (1846); one of the first Gothic buildings.

plainer styles were thought inadequate. However, AWN Pugin's pure, structurally honest Early English design preferences, John Ruskin's Gothic principles of polychromy and arcaded exteriors, and William Burges's medieval muscular style – derived from the Gothic styles of Italy, France and the Low Countries – were the ingredients utilized by architects active in Bombay in the 19th century. Their proposals and designs put the city firmly on the world stage.

Prior to the 1840s, prominent buildings constructed in Bombay, such as St Andrew's or the Scottish Kirk (1818), the Mint (1829), and the Town Hall (1833), were customarily in the neo-Classical style. However, the city's architecture took a new direction as its urban centre started to rapidly grow with causeways to the mainland built in 1835. Land at the southern or Colaba end of the island was reclaimed then too, and the Great Indian Peninsula Railway (now known as the Central Railway) opened the section to Thane in 1853.

Two health care facilities, the Sir Jamsetjee Jeejeebhoy Hospital and the Grant Medical College, both designed by unknown architects, were Bombay's first experiments with the neo-Gothic style. Significantly, each was constructed in a mixture of brick and rubble stone faced with *chunam* (lime stucco), following the style of the city's early neo-Classical buildings. The hospital opened in 1846, although it began in 1834 as a dispensary. The original hospital building is now demolished, and the Grant Medical College is in a state of serious disrepair.

AFGHAN MEMORIAL CHURCH

In 1844, Henry Bartle Edward Frere proclaimed his vision of Bombay as *Urbs Prima in Indis*, or India's first city, and the developing metropolis adopted the motto. Appointed in 1842 as the young private secretary to the governor of Bombay, Frere saw the need to change the city's image together with its function. He also expressed a desire, fuelled perhaps by the death of his brother Richard on the battlefield in 1843, to commemorate the victims of the Afghan War. The glory of the British empire, to which so many soldiers had sacrificed their lives, was to be memorialized in a fine new stone church.

In the same year, Frere sailed to Britain to marry. While there, he carefully observed the most current architectural work in the country. The development of the neo-Gothic Afghan Memorial Church, or the Church of St John the Evangelist, was begun at this time. The process began with a series of complimentary proposed plans despatched to Bombay through an application to the Architectural Society of Oxford. The designs were accompanied with financial support, but the proposals were all considered too expensive, despite alternative cheaper construction materials being considered as well. Then, in 1847, Frere approached the Society again, on behalf of the church's trustees, and he succeeded in bringing back to Bombay drawings by George Gilbert Scott, one of Britain's most distinguished and prolific neo-Gothic designers. St John's was the first building in Bombay for which designs were sought from an architect practising abroad. Regrettably, Scott's now lost designs were also deemed too elaborate and expensive for Bombay. However, the British architect and engineer, Henry Conybeare, in Bombay to design the city's water supply system, shared with Frere an abiding interest in the Gothic style. Both men embraced the theories of the Ecclesiological Society that sought to impose a rigorous and 'pure' style of neo-Gothic upon church architecture. The result of their collaboration had far-reaching consequences, as it irrevocably set the neo-Gothic trend in Bombay for the next 30 years. Although Conybeare's professional qualifications focused upon engineering, he possessed an extensive knowledge of medieval architecture and was anxious to find patrons for his designs. In Bombay, he offered the additional advantage of on-site architectural supervision while he promised economical construction costs. These two advantages helped win him the church commission, though final costs for the building did run considerably higher than his original estimates.

The Afghan Church is the largest and most elaborate of Conybeare's architectural compositions. According to Frere, it "owes some of its best features" to GG Scott's original designs. An excellent example of Gothic Revival architecture, it was 35 per cent cheaper to construct than the neo-Classical buildings of the era. The church opened in 1858, eleven years after construction first began. General John Augustus Fuller supervised completion of the church during Conybeare's absence in Britain from 1850 to 1854. Later, upon his return, Conybeare became involved with the waterworks project and could spare little time for the church. So, Fuller went on to design the reredos, the vestry on the north side of the church, the entrance porch and the weather vane.

In 1865, the government granted Rs 38,644 for the addition of a spire. This not only enhanced the grandeur of St John's and provided for a peal of bells, but it also made the church

St John's Church built in stone in neo-Gothic style.

stand out as a landmark. That responded to another need, according to the terms of the original lease, as the deed specified that the land west of the church was to always remain open, providing ships approaching Bombay an unobstructed view of the spire.

Imported stained glass windows were first seen in Bombay at St John's Church. The original set of 42 panels depicts a range of biblical themes funded entirely by private contributions to the church and located around the side aisles and also in the main chancel window. Here, one of the notable lancet lights has *Abraham and Isaac* at the lowest level, followed by *The Crucifixion*, and *Our Lord in Majesty and Power*. William Wailes designed the stained glass in the lancet windows. He had earlier collaborated with William Butterfield on London's Church of St Barnabas, to which *The Bombay Builder* favourably compared St John's. Capturing the refining influences of the Gothic Revival, St Barnabas was admired for studiously avoiding bright mid-Victorian industrial finishes.

Butterfield designed some of the railings and the benches, seats, choir stalls, entrance screen, and the floor-paving pattern for the Minton tiles imported from Britain. To economize, alterations were made to some features of Butterfield's original drawings, including ironwork commissioned from Bombay's Sir Jamsetjee Jeejeebhoy School of Art. Parts of Butterfield's scheme were completed as late as 1903 and the chancel screen was only finished and installed in 1928.

The cost of the church, including later embellishments, was estimated at Rs 210,895, of which just a little over half was borne by the government. Of the initial Rs 70,000 needed to start construction, the government granted only 30,000, together with the Rs 15,000 raised by the sale of the incomplete Kaira Church. Private contributions amounted to Rs 25,000. HBE Frere's Rs 500 contribution was notable, but Sir Cowasjee Jehangier Readymoney's donation of Rs 7,500 was the largest

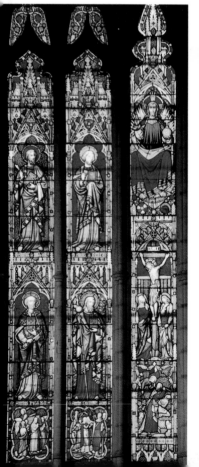

single private contribution to the building fund. A successful Parsi banker of Bombay who rose from godown keeper to guarantees broker for two British firms, Readymoney (1812-78) felt it was important to complete the Afghan Memorial Church for patriotic reasons. He was one of several Parsis renowned for their interest in civic affairs and charitable endeavours in the 19th century.

Conybeare's church exemplifies his preference for the clarity and simplicity of Early English Gothic design. Early English was the style most promoted by the architect and theorist AWN Pugin as 'correct' church architecture. However, in Bombay, St John's broke not only stylistic but structural ground as well. By rejecting the *chunam* facings of earlier buildings, Conybeare was the first architect to use coursed Kurla stone and buff-coloured basalt for the exterior, and Porbandar stone for the interior piers and arches. The natural finishes of these stones weathered extremely well in Bombay's climate, requiring minimal maintenance. Thus, Conybeare's architectural experiment

Stained glass by William Wailes in chancel lancet windows.

was found to be such an economical approach, that his solution was adopted throughout the developing city. Bombay's nearby stone became an alternative to the painted surfaces so liable to be ravaged by humidity and the ferocious monsoon rain. In this way Conybeare's church, a prototype of stone building materials, established itself as highly influential in a city about to determine its own architectural style. The involvement of so many other distinguished contributors in its construction only served to amplify the importance of the church's novel style and made its handsome final appearance more memorable.

Interior view of St John's with ironwork, chancel's stained glass windows and high altar (right). Detail of high altar and reredos; note fine marble inlay and Gothic features (below).

SIR JAMSETJEE JEEJEEBHOY SCHOOL OF ART –
A SCHOOL FOR THE STYLE

A Parsi merchant prince of Bombay reinforced Bartle Frere's vision of an urban Bombay decorated in the neo-Gothic style. With a fortune made in the China trade, Jamsetjee Jeejeebhoy spent a total of £350,000 on 'public benefactions' from 1824 to 1854. Knighted in 1855 for his exceptional philanthropy, he was made the first Indian baronet two years later by Queen Victoria. His statue, sculpted by Carlo Marochetti, stands in the Asiatic Society of Bombay, Central Library (old Town Hall). Jeejeebhoy was more than an astute and well-travelled businessman. He understood the potential of Indian products in the evolving industrialized world.

Portrait of the philanthropist, Sir Jamsetjee Jeejeebhoy.

Simultaneously, he realised that Indian manufacturing techniques could not hope to keep pace with the West. He resolved to restore, reform and maintain the ancient crafts of India, and offered the government Rs 100,000 in 1855 to found a school along the lines of Alexander Hunter's art school in Madras (now known as Chennai). Its aim would be to teach painting, drawing, design, ornamental pottery, metal and wood carving and turning, "wherein the user of complicated machinery is not indispensable," and gem and pebble cutting. The approach taken would shape designs around the cornerstone of industrial production while nurturing the unique qualities of Indian design so as to combine them with Western techniques. After the school's early success in recording the Ajanta frescoes, for those unable to visit them, the institution gained government sponsorship and official recognition. In the decades that followed, the teachers and students of the Sir Jamsetjee Jeejeebhoy (JJ) School of Art decorated Bombay's Gothic Revival buildings with sculptural and wrought iron details.

The school's founding committee, of which Henry Conybeare was a member, was drawn from the organizers of the Indian pavilion at London's Great Exhibition (Crystal Palace) of 1851. The committee were aware of the competition posed by British products to traditional Indian crafts, especially in the marketing of cloth and pottery. It was hoped the teachers of the new school, appointed in Britain, would remedy the situation, while teaching a wide variety of courses in the arts. The first arrivals were

GW Terry, who taught painting; MJ Higgins, the ironworker; and the sculptor John Lockwood Kipling whose son, the renowned writer Rudyard Kipling was born within the school premises in 1865. Other experienced and influential artists followed.

In the early years, London's Science and Art Museum planned the school's courses, and Bombay's Mechanics' Institute was combined with the JJ School. This was because both came to be seen as sharing a common purpose: to engineer, design and adorn new structures planned for the growing city. The JJ School displayed a marked success in developing this role as the 19th century progressed, and today it continues to offer diplomas in architecture.

The JJ's classes first began at the Elphinstone Institution in 1857. In 1865 the Ramparts Removal Committee, responsible for new building in the developing city, offered the JJ School its present site on Hornby Road (Dr Dadabhai Naoroji Road). Although several reputed architects were invited to submit designs, William Burges, the well-known British architect with a pervasive interest in the decorative arts, was

Rear view of Burges's proposal for JJ School of Art (1866); note large overhanging eaves, arcades, smithy with chimneys.

considered a natural for the commission. His design became legend in architectural circles for "compelling rigid thirteenth-century Gothic to fulfil the requirements of the torrid zone." Burges was influenced primarily by the buildings of Italy and Constantinople, as well as suggestions from the architects, Thomas Roger Smith and Owen Jones, who were familiar with Bombay and probably suggested the "flat double roofs with deep eaves, and lintels fit for window blinds".

William Emerson, a student of Burges, accompanied the proposal's 129 drawings of the school to Bombay. In this "most marvellous design that he ever made", Burges had provided for a building that was "at once compact and roomy", fairly simple in its interior plan, and suited to Bombay's conditions. It was, in the architectural historian Joseph M Crook's words, "essentially practical", and it greatly influenced subsequent architectural design in Victorian Bombay. Corridors provided a plan with double walls, and slabs of pierced stone (or *jalis*) and small windows excluded much of the sun's glare and yet admitted air freely. The *jalis* were a direct reference to Mughal building practices. Burges was probably introduced to them through TC Hope's published photographs or the Indian display at the Great Exhibition. Burges also proposed a vaulted floor, raised on a terrace, as a safeguard against monsoon flooding, and a domed smithy that would have added a spectacular 13th century French Gothic touch to Bombay. Particularly admired by Bombay's architects and planners was the decorative elaboration for the exterior surface of the building, which included corbelled balconies and open bay windows.

The plans were ultimately abandoned, a great loss to the city.

Front view of Burges's proposal for JJ School of Art (1866); note central staircase tower, corner turrets, overhanging eaves, arcaded corridors, self-contained garden compound with fountains.

Apart from being considered too expensive to execute, an unfortunate disagreement arose over the standard 2.5 per cent fee paid by the Public Works Department (PWD) for engineering work. Burges expected a commission of at least 5 per cent for his architectural designs. Eventually, he was paid over Rs 15,630 for his drawings of the school building. An affront to Burges and his *métier*, the argument proved detrimental to Bombay's reputation in British architectural circles, and probably contributed to the decline of designs offered by architects abroad. Bombay's financial collapse in 1865 may also have generated a wariness of projects destined for the city.

Construction of the JJ School of Art began eight years after Emerson submitted Burges's proposal. George Twigge Molecey's design incorporated some of the features proposed by Burges, Smith and Jones, and may also have drawn on features of the South Kensington School of

Art. Molecey's large double-storeyed central hall and studios minimally suggest the E-shape of Burges's original proposal. Two staircases from the hall lead to spacious studio rooms. The school's southern façade is fully articulated with a wide and airy outer corridor where students can sit and look out over the garden. It also shields the wall most likely to be heated by the sun. However, the decorative scheme of the building is rather pedestrian – simple arched corridors, and engaged columns with floriated

poppoi capitals at the side of each opening. Square cut Kurla stone was used for construction, trimmed with buff and red Vasai stone. The roofing is of red ceramic tiles, and there are large plate glass windows in the northern studios. The rest of the fenestration combines shutters and windows, with wrought iron grilles providing security.

John Fuller was the superintending engineer and his assistant was Khan Bahadur Muncherjee Cowasjee Murzban. The facility took over three years to construct and opened in 1878.

Benedictine kitchen, Marmoutier, France (left), upon which Burges based the smithy in his JJ School proposal. Modern view of Molecey's 1874-78 garden elevation, JJ School of Art (below).

GOVERNOR FRERE'S PLAN

Appointed governor of Bombay in 1862, Frere demolished the obsolete fort walls that same year. The dramatic change made room for his comprehensive vision of a modern city. Frere's strongly-held views on suitable city architecture were delivered in no uncertain terms at the Royal Architectural Museum. Recorded in *The Building News* of 1870, his speech reads like the manifesto of a reformer. He openly criticized his 18th century forbears for generating "acres of featureless streets" that were dull and extremely repetitive, referring specifically to the heart of Georgian London. According to Frere, the city fabric called for something more personal and invigorating, appealing in its very complexity. He felt equal disdain for the structures in British India constructed up till then. Frere's term as governor ended in 1867, but several events occurred around the period of his governorship to speed Bombay on the road to success. The city established railway links with the heart of India, several cotton mills were founded with the latest steam-powered technology, and the Suez Canal made Bombay easily accessible to the 19th century power centres and manufacturing capabilities of Europe.

By odd coincidence, just prior to the commencement of Frere's term, there was a blockade of the southern ports during the American Civil War. This resulted in an overwhelming British demand for Indian cotton, as American cotton was unavailable for British mills. While Bombay rode the crest of this economic wave from 1861 to 1865, its newly prosperous mercantile class indulged in extensive property speculation, which later financed several land reclamation schemes. This dovetailed well with Frere's own architectural schemes for the city. A financial crash in Bombay, which came with the end of the war in America, only temporarily foiled Bombay's development plans, as the city's commercial future was assured by the Suez Canal and its own strategically placed harbour facilities. Even just a decade after the US Civil War ended, the port city could yield £3,000,000 in tax revenue to Britain's treasury.

The development of Bombay in the 1860s was both contemporaneous and comparable to Napoleon III's rebuilding of Paris, London's extensive sewerage

Frere's coat of arms depicted in stained glass, University Convocation Hall.

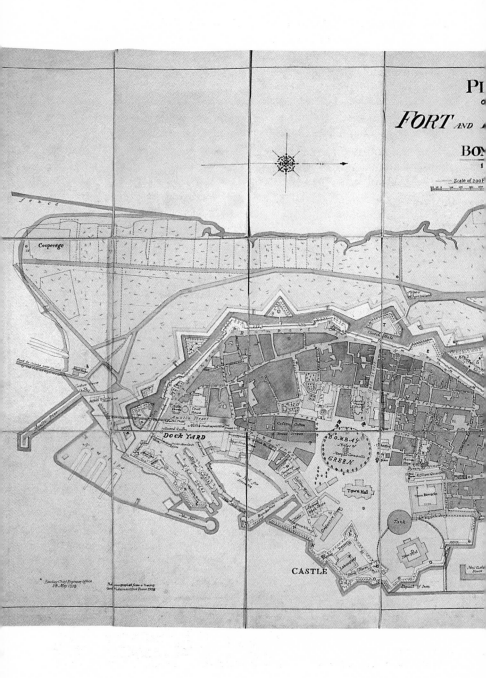

P[
o[
FORT AND [
BOM[

Scale of 700 F[

Cooperage

DOCK YARD

BOMBAY
or
GREEN

Town Hall

Tank

CASTLE

British Architects (RIBA), professor at University College, London, and an influential member of the Architectural Association, he was able to arouse the interest of prominent British architects in Bombay's building projects. As mentioned, GG Scott and Burges were amongst the more famous practitioners of Gothic architecture in Britain who submitted drawings to Bombay. However, Smith's connections with the Science and Art Department in South Kensington also brought him into contact with several young aspiring architects of promise, whom he nominated for service in Bombay.

Smith himself also designed a European General Hospital for Bombay, in collaboration with Matthew Digby Wyatt and Owen Jones. Smith spent the period of 1864-65 in Bombay with the purpose of overseeing its construction. Acquiring a close familiarity with Bombay's conditions, he realised that his preference for the Gothic style had to be tempered by local requirements. Rooms were to be spacious, well ventilated, and yet screened from the strong sun. Thick external walls were essential and were to be lined by verandas at every storey. Verandas could be the most useful feature of a building as they allowed for architectural decoration, such as corbels, projections and breaks, and provided a centre for various kinds of activity. He also detailed the use of flooring as a cooling surface if sprinkled with water, and the need to build verandas of light but weather-resistant materials.

Smith was advocating and attempting to define an Anglo-Indian style of architecture, modelled on Gothic Revival forms, but using Indian materials and craftsmen and adapted to Indian conditions. In this he followed Frere's ideal of creating an indigenous school of architecture "as extensive and as distinct as the pure Hindu and Mahometan schools of former days". Visibly successful in Bombay, this intended Anglo-Indian style failed to travel across the country.

Another aspect of Frere's ingenious scheme was the way he financed his projects.

Elevation line drawing of university clock tower and library.

and water improvements, and Vienna's construction of the Ringstrasse on the site of its old fort walls. At a ceremony to mark the start of the Bombay Fort's demolition, Governor Frere detailed his plan for the modern city. It is clear that Frere saw himself as master planner, civic improver and empire builder all in one. The buildings he required were meant to enhance the government's image, and enable it to expand its services and rule more effectively.

Housing and public services in the British empire's second most populous city were in need of improvement. Not as rich as many cities in the West, health needs would normally have received lower priority than commercial or economic development. But, Bombay owed its efficient infrastructure to Frere's administrative vision, and he transformed both the civic role and the appearance of the city.

Frere drew up a list of fourteen buildings "to meet the most pressing wants of the military and civil administration." It comprised a barracks, a hospital, a high court, a small causes court, a police magistrates court, post and telegraph offices, a customs house, quarters for government officers, a secretariat, a station for the Great Indian Peninsula Railway, school rooms attached to several churches, a treasury building, a records office, and offices for various government departments. To this list were later appended university buildings and an art school.

HBE Frere (above). *Bombay Fort in 1827* (facing pages).

The Ramparts Removal Committee was the official entity formed to provide guidelines and to oversee new government construction. In an unprecedented move, established leaders of architectural fashion were brought to Bombay to advise and assist in the planning of the city. This committee of architects and engineers functioned under the direction of James Trubshawe. Descended from a well-known line of Staffordshire architects, he arrived in Bombay in 1863 as Architectural Secretary to the government. Trubshawe was further assisted by the astute move of the British government to amalgamate the PWD and the Royal Engineers into one service. The Royal Engineers had, in the 1860s, the most extensive experience of India's construction needs, which they then shared with their PWD colleagues, many of them eager to secure future careers in town planning and architecture.

TR Smith was responsible with Trubshawe for defining the ground rules of Bombay's architecture. As lecturer at the Royal Institute of

Various colours and textures of stone that can be seen on Bombay's Gothic buildings.

Through an unprecedented series of imperial grants to the Bombay Special Fund, he more than doubled the annual amounts of money available for public spending, particularly in the period 1862-67. Bombay thereby came to "boast of numerous buildings, which certainly have no equal in any town or city of India, and which will stand comparison with those to be found in…any other part of the world." It took only a little more than 30 years for Frere's 'High Victorian dream' to materialize. In the process, a distinctly Anglo-Indian architectural style evolved, comprising pure Victorian architecture with a strong Indian component, well suited to Bombay's climate.

The Gothic style that developed at Bombay most easily harmonized with historic Indian preferences for sculptured balconies and an eclectic range of interiors and exteriors. The style offered the colour and complexity of Mughal and Hindu architecture, and it appealed to local benefactors. This was an important consideration as Parsis, who were estimated in 1855 to own about half of Bombay, including substantial parts of the Fort and Malabar Hill neighbourhoods, Jain cotton brokers, philanthropic Banias, and Bhatia Shets often sponsored the public buildings in 19th century Bombay. As landlords and benefactors, the Gothic skylines, turrets, and circular and oval windows were closer in appearance to traditional Indian 'palace architecture' than the neo-Classical style, the Gothic's alternative. In addition, Gothic Revival architects in Bombay were able to capitalize on the extensive variety of fine building stone available nearby. The durable local blue basalt and red basalt from Pune, or a buff-coloured Kurla stone provided an attractive structural material either for walls or the inner sections of a building. Tough and unsuited to fine carving when used in construction, the basalt was commonly left 'roughly dressed', asserting a distinctively masculine finish. The hardness of these stones also made them excellent candidates for foundations. Other stone varieties employed were off-white Porbandar and red Vasai sandstones, both of which proved excellent for carving and decorative accents. In addition, stone from Kutch also offered a wide range of colours and types, and Ratnagiri had a distinctive grey granite, to list but some of the many stones available.

WATSON'S HOTEL – CAST IRON ARCHITECTURE

One more highly significant imported architectural design type of the 1860s should be considered here: cast iron architecture. The British engineer Rowland Mason Ordish designed, manufactured and shipped to Bombay an entire hotel. The construction of pre-fabricated buildings was in its infancy at this date, and in the case of Watson's Hotel, on Esplanade (now Mahatma Gandhi) Road, an exceptional building for Bombay was the result. The project furthers our understanding of the architectural experiments taking place in Bombay, but in completely different materials and in an approach utterly at odds with Burges's vision. Ordish's design for Watson's Hotel was a superlative example of a fully rigid, skeleton-framed building with a structure fabricated entirely of cast iron. There were several important cast iron buildings proposed for the city, but only this one structure was built and remains in Bombay. It is also architecturally the most significant.

The hotel commission most likely grew out of collaboration on the Iron Kiosk project, designed by Jones and manufactured by Andrew Handyside & Co of Derby. Intended for Bombay, the kiosk languished in London for unknown reasons. Erected in the Royal Horticultural Society Gardens, South Kensington, it was never shipped to India. However, the kiosk was a *tour-de-force* of iron working and casting and it used a diagonal roof grid construction. The joints of the roof were dovetailed and

The elegant cast iron and covered arcade of Watson's Hotel; engraving from the late 1860s.

disguised by Jones's decorative scheme. This method enabled the exterior supporting columns to be of uniform width throughout the perimeter of the structure. The kiosk had a 'double roof' to allow hot air to escape through the clerestory windows, a method described and suggested by the architectural consultant to Bombay, TR Smith. Such a design directly related to the many efforts made to 'foil the heat' of India: through ventilators, iron roof constructions and open spaces between roof and wall, in addition to other 'thermantidotes', as they were called then. All of these techniques had varying degrees of effectiveness. However, none proved as spectacular as its claims purported, and Jones's suggestion of "cascades of iron roofs" was only one of many proposed themes in this area of research. But, through the construction of the kiosk, Ordish made his contact with India, having worked with Jones since 1851, when they were both engaged on the erection of the Crystal Palace, London. Ordish was surely given the Watson's Hotel commission through his connection to these earlier projects.

Watson's Hotel, like the Iron Kiosk, was especially adapted to Bombay's climate, and its site – at the time of construction – possessed a superb situation, now lost in the muddle of a more modern Bombay. Built on ground acquired by the removal of the ramparts, it formerly commanded "fine open views of the Esplanade, sea, Back Bay, and Malabar Hill to the

Jones's Iron Kiosk proposed for Bombay; note double roof for ventilation and decorative cresting.

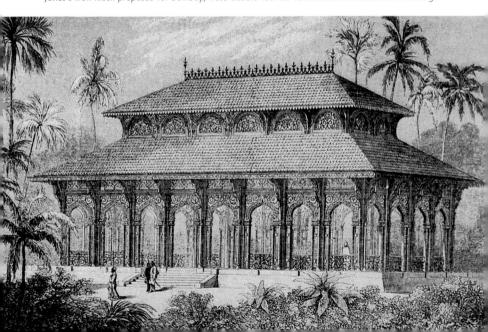

west; Matheran and the Ghaut Range of hills to the north; and of the grand harbour to the east."

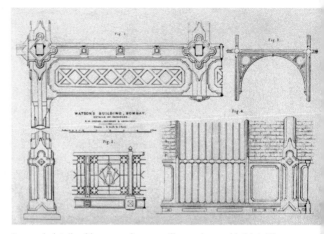

Ironwork details of beams, columns, grilles, arches and brick infill.

The building, erected in late 1868 or early 1869 and opened in early 1871, was soon known as the Esplanade Hotel. Its totally pre-fabricated cast iron skeletal structure, with brick non-load bearing insertions, was a novelty for Bombay. Now it is believed that the structure is also an internationally significant breakthrough design, of some consequence to the world, for both the novelty of its engineering and its very early use of these building technologies. The building was formed of cast columns, bressumers and wrought iron girders that tied these elements together and formed the floors. The spaces on the elevation, divided by columns into bays, are filled in with brickwork, but only a half-brick thick. Each bay also has windows, framed in metal mullions and transoms, to support the thin surrounding brickwork. The window glass is covered with the Venetian louvres, common to Eastern buildings, allowing for a construction module that affords the greatest opportunity for the most thorough ventilation of the building. Both the ironwork and bricks for this project originated from James Hatwood's firm of Derby and suggestions as to the plan of the structure are attributed to John Hudson Watson himself, a tailor and the hotelier.

The structure was an interesting and clever attempt at building quickly and easily in a country where on-site supervision posed many problems and frustrations for imported designs. As a pre-fabricated manufactured construction, it had many enticing qualities worthy of trial. Requiring few local materials, it was insect- and weather-proof, and easy to erect.

In the Crystal Palace and other earlier prototypes, pre-fabrication had made possible quick and inexpensive shelter without large foundations or specially trained labour. So for Ordish, an engineer, to build in this manner was a logical choice. Bombay desperately needed a comfortable hotel at this period, and Watson's was meant to be a low cost 'modern' solution. Frere's connection with the iron trade, through his father's researches and business undertakings, may have encouraged such a structure's arrival in Bombay, but too few records remain to retrace the history and forces behind the commission.

Unsympathetically cluttered with offices today, Watson's Hotel comprises a central block and two wings, measuring 188 by 80 feet (approximately 57.3 by 24.4 metres). The wings are symmetrical each having 30 feet of frontage, and the central block with the main staircase is 45 feet wide. A building of five storeys, the first storey's ceiling is 20 feet high, with the ceiling heights reduced on each succeeding storey. A large well or atrium, 120 by 20 feet, incorporated into the central block of the building, originally offered increased ventilation.

Watson's Hotel circa 1880s; view showing ground-floor arcades.

For luxury, the building was pre-eminent in the city. Shops, wine cellars and storerooms occupied the ground floor. Also on the ground floor were a commodious bar, refreshment rooms, and six billiard tables. The shops benefited from the protective mass of the overhanging building as it provided convenient covered arcades for potential customers to browse out of the sun and sheltered from the rain. The arcade was another first for Bombay, and it was an idea that became hugely successful and imitated all along Esplanade Road.

The "finest and handsomest" dining room in Bombay was located on the hotel's first floor, and it could accommodate an orchestra of thirty. There were several smaller rooms for private parties, a public drawing room, a special room for ladies and a coffee room. The three upper floors contained 130 rooms and 20 suites, the ones on the top floor being reserved for gentlemen. Open courtyards lined by deep verandas facilitated the flow of air within the guest chambers. The interiors of the rooms were finished in teak and mahogany, and Minton tiles paved the floors. The luxurious hotel added much elegance to the city and was a financial success. An annexe was erected in 1888 to Robert Fellowes Chisholm's design, a short walk away, behind the old Royal Bombay Yacht Club, but it is now demolished. The Watson's Hotel building is today Mahendra Mansion, and every possible space has been filled and subdivided.

HIGH GOTHIC DREAM

A VICTORIAN VISION REALISED

FRERE TOWN

'Frere Town' is the term used for the 'new' civic buildings constructed within, around and really upon the precincts occupied hitherto by the old fort walls. The 'High Gothic dream' that Bombay fulfils comprises a complete series of planned and densely grouped public buildings of similar style, scale and materials. These buildings may not be of as high a design standard as the masterpieces of individual practitioners in Britain, but the ensemble, considered as a group, is unrivalled in the world. There is no

other city with so many buildings erected in similar style, with so few modern insertions. The grandeur and completeness of the undertaking is breathtaking. The buildings present a spectacular skyline, easily appreciated by standing in the largest open green spaces of the city centre, today's Oval, Cross and Azad Maidans. From there one can observe the rows of façades and the skyline formed by the group. The buildings' luxurious materials and fine craftsmanship boldly exude the confidence of the Victorian age. They incorporate some of the most advanced architectural work of the time in their design and external expression, and constitute

architectural treasures of the international neo-Gothic movement. The historical basis for their appearance should be clearly understood as derived from the study of medieval European buildings. Yet, the group also reveals significant input from Frere's Victorian neo-Gothic concepts of a 'correct' cityscape.

Although many of the buildings were completed long after Frere's return to Britain in 1867, he would have agreed that they admirably translated his vision of Anglo-Indian architecture into stone and built form.

Skyline evoking Frere's High Gothic dream with the High Court, Oriental Buildings and BMC offices.

THE SECRETARIAT

Construction began in 1867 on the Secretariat, the
first building in the series lining the Oval Maidan,
and now referred to as the 'old' Secretariat. General
Henry St Clair Wilkins was asked to design an
imposing and important urban symbol for Bombay. In
both size and expense it was his most ambitious
project, faithful to the design recommendations of
TR Smith. The Secretariat was the first structure
designed and erected by the PWD from its own
department's resources, and it became a paradigm for
subsequent work Bombay. It opened in 1874.

The Secretariat faces west, to benefit from breezes
off the sea, which was considerably closer to the
building at the time of construction. Indeed, the
majority of buildings at the edge of the *maidan* face
west, with the length of their rooms running north to south. Setbacks,
iron awnings and polychromatic arcades of stonework articulate the wide
main façade. Wilkins intentionally made the building narrow to enable
breezes to penetrate every part of the structure, aided by airy spiral
staircases at either end. The central tower is 170 feet high and rises above
a large cantilevered central staircase. Blue basalt rubble was used for
construction faced with roughly dressed buff-coloured Kurla basalt in 7 to
8 inch (17-20 cm) courses. The polychromatic stonework was obtained by
using buff-coloured Porbandar stone, Kurla stone, local blue basalt, Pune
red basalt, Ransome's Patent Stone (a cast stone used here for the first
time in Bombay) and Hemnagar silicious sandstone, all neatly finished.
Blue basalt and buff Porbandar were employed for corridor arches on the
ground floor, red basalt and buff Porbandar on the first floor, and the
outer cornice of the second floor used Ransome's Stone. Hemnagar stone
was reserved for use on capitals, cornices and small corridor shafts.
Terracotta Broomhall tiles roofed the structure over teakwood joists and
planking, and Minton tiles paved the floors. The building was partially
fireproof, with floors supported by iron girders infilled with concrete
sounding under the tiles, or with concrete poured over Porbandar stone –
a novelty for Bombay that reveals the engineering interests and ingenuity
of the architect. This was the first public building to pursue a completely
neo-Gothic decorative scheme that included John Adams's furniture
designs, executed by the PWD in teak inlaid with blackwood.

The prominent *porte-cochère* (carriage porch) bears Governor Frere's
coat of arms, a lasting tribute to his vision for Bombay and its governance.

The Secretariat by Wilkins was the first in Frere's line of Gothic buildings on the Esplanade, facing west over the Oval Maidan; note the long and flat façade, central staircase tower and arcades.

The Secretariat functioned adequately until the 1950s, when a new building was constructed on land associated with the Nariman Point reclamation. Wilkins's project employed Indian craftsmen and it used local materials wherever possible, successfully establishing that these were sources the government could rely upon. Frere earnestly desired to abandon the import of materials and expertise from Britain, and thereby avoid running the risk of unnecessary disappointment and expense through possible damage in transit and misunderstood orders.

As the first building to attempt construction on this scale and in the prescribed manner of TR Smith *et al*, the Secretariat should be viewed as a success. Although by no means the most beautiful building in the city, its solid construction was innovative and carefully detailed. The building's functional and heavy appearance would have been admired at the time as 'true to nature', a doctrine highly regarded by the contemporary Pre-Raphaelite movement in Britain. If there are flaws in the Secretariat's design, they are more obvious at a distance. It is then that the long and unbroken façade reveals the architect's unfamiliarity with proportion, a skill that remains one of the most difficult to master. The government may also have specifically asked for a long flat façade, as this would provide a floor plan to match those of the adjacent university and the High Court. On the other hand, the rich sculptural embellishments would have earned the admiration of even contemporary architects practising in Britain.

UNIVERSITY BUILDINGS

The University Convocation Hall, the University Library and the Rajabai Tower form the finest group of buildings facing Back Bay, and are excellent examples of GG Scott's work. Sir CJ Readymoney was the first to contribute a generous Rs 100,000 in April 1863, followed by Premchand Roychund, a cotton, securities and commodities broker of the Jain community, whose donations over the next few years came to a munificent sum of Rs 839,000, most of which was spent on the University Library and clock tower.

The site, in the centre of a row of structures that starts with the Secretariat and ends with the High Court, gives the university pride of place. After Scott's plans were assessed, an unusually large plot was demarcated and the street plan was altered to accommodate a loose quadrangle. The group of buildings was designed in the ornamental French style of the 13th century, and made intentional reference to European universities. Their ecclesiastical appearance reinforced the

1880s' view of the Convocation Hall, library and clock tower with Back Bay in the distance.

historically Christian and reforming role of universities. The buildings'
merits are further exemplified when contrasted with the neighbouring less
refined compositions. Facing west and surrounded by gardens, the
university complex dignifies the city and creates highly
serviceable areas for study and research. In a 1952
expansion of classroom facilities, and in accordance with
the original plan, a neo-Gothic but unsympathetically
austere structure closed the eastern side of the quadrangle
and its garden aspect.

By the time construction began on the university at
the very end of 1868, GT Molecey, Walter Paris, and
General Fuller had adapted the designs to Indian
requirements and materials. Molecey oversaw the
ironwork required for the project, and made the detailed
drawings for construction. Heaton, Butler & Bayne Ltd
of London provided the stained glass and leaded lights,
and the roof tiles were from Taylor, also of London.
Minton tiles were employed on the paved surfaces.

The two-storey University
Library, with the most complex
plan of the group, provides a 152-
foot wide horizontal backdrop to
the Rajabai Tower. The tower, built
abutting and adjacent to the library,
has large pointed arch openings in
its base to provide the library's
porte-cochère. The library building's
delicate and attenuated scale is
enhanced by the juxtaposition and
interplay of surfaces: the tower's
base is finished in rough but
beautifully coloured Kurla stone
with Porbandar additions, while the
dominant finish on the library
façade is smoothly cut Porbandar
stone. A delicately patterned screen
of this material is also employed
along the length of the main

The library's stone staircase and leaded lights
(right). *Carved stone dog as newel post* (top).

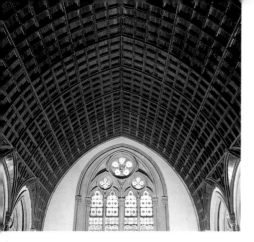

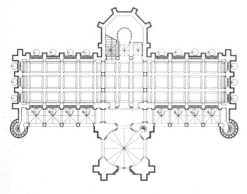

western façade. Its capping balustrade is joined at either end by spiral staircases terminating in conical feather-cut patterned roofs. The plant depicted on the ground floor capitals belongs to either the melon or the castor oil family. The stone surrounds of the round windows on the first floor, carved with floriated multifoil details, have stained glass inserts. Arcades 14 feet deep on both floors help capture the westerly breezes from the sea.

Scott designed a groin-vaulted ground floor entrance hall with a large reception counter on the right. Two lecture rooms were separated from this main hall by wooden screens, each with stained-glass inserts rendered in a Gothic Revival 'banqueting hall' style. The central staircase is placed to the left of the reception desk. Walking up from the ground floor, where two cross arches spring from a capital, the visitor catches sight of the carved heads of Homer and Shakespeare. The staircase also has a vaulted ceiling lit by large lancet stained glass windows, which face east, and richly carved animals decorate its balcony at the second-storey landing. It then leads to the teakwood vaulted hall of the large reading room.

This reading room has a 32-foot high ceiling, and is lit from the

Teakwood ceiling of reading room (top). *Floor plan of University Library* (centre). *Screen in 'banqueting hall' style with stained glass* (left).

north and south by large stone
Early English bar-tracery windows,
and from the east and west through
a series of large pointed-arch
windows, shaded by an arcade on
the west. To echo the bulge of the
staircase on the eastern façade, a
large space was cleverly inserted
within the clock tower so as not to
be externally visible, with the *porte-
cochère* placed beneath, and the
tower above this room. With Early
English bar-tracery fenestration on
three sides, it successfully merges
the clock tower with the library,
visually and in function. The
woodwork and bookcases fit into a
harmonious neo-Gothic decorative
scheme. Major Charles Mant
(1839-81), the superintending

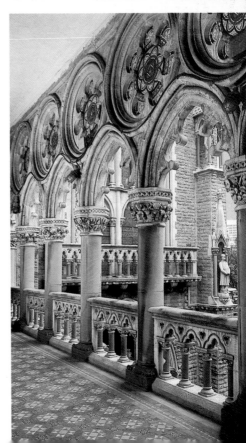

*Neo-Gothic Venetian style arcade in GG Scott's
University Library (right). Compare with 14th-
15th century Palazzo Ducale, Venice (top).*

architect, advised against a proposal during construction to gild the teak ceiling, as he felt it would prove not only impractical but also too costly.

The Rajabai Tower, dedicated to Premchand Roychund's mother, took nine years to complete. The design source cited for the structure was Giotto's unbuilt proposal for the bell tower adjacent to the Duomo in Florence. In detail and balance it also compares well with its predecessor, Big Ben of London. Bombay University's clock tower is 280 feet high and consists of seven storeys. Soaring 120 feet above its neighbouring buildings, the Rajabai Tower was, for a while, the tallest structure in the city. The sculptures on its four sides represent 24 'castes' of western India, and stand within niches or sit under canopies of crocketed pinnacle forms of varying neo-Gothic designs, which are exquisitely sculpted from Porbandar stone and well proportioned for their site. Forming decorative pinnacles at the top of the tower, the canopies support the buttresses holding the octagonal crocketed lantern that terminates the composition. The sculptures remain in excellent condition, despite their age.

The tower's four-sided clock became operational in February 1880,

although the rest of the structure was completed three years earlier. The fourth floor of the tower contains the clock's mechanism. The opal glass dials, which display the time, are 12 feet 6 inches in diameter, and can be illuminated at night, originally by gas jets placed behind them. The corner balconies below the dials were intended as viewing points. Lund & Blockley designed the works and carillons, programmed to play sixteen different tunes. John Taylor & Co, Leicestershire,

Premchand Roychund, the clock tower's donor (top left). His mother, Rajabai, for whom the tower is named (top right). Mechanism of clock showing pendulum, escapement and wheel work (left). Elevation of library and clock tower (facing page).

manufactured the sixteen bells, the largest weighing three tons. The bell frame, designed by General Hyde of the Railway Department, was made by Westwood Bailey & Co.

The Sir Cowasjee Jehangier Convocation Hall, begun in 1869 and initially known as the University Senate Hall, cost a total of Rs 400,000 when it opened in 1874. It stands about a hundred feet to the south of the library, and has a rectangular ground plan with an apse attached to the southern end of the hall, and a porch and staircase added to the northern façade. The hall, designed to seat a thousand people on its main floor and gallery, is built of the same materials as the library, with the addition of grey granite from Ratnagiri for the staircase pillars, and Chinese marble used in conjunction with Minton tiling for the flooring of the central aisle and apsidal southern end.

The exterior provides a complex but pleasing arrangement of neo-Gothic forms, both complementary to and competitive with its neighbour. The eastern and western elevations are identical, and each has setback buttressing rising up to the second floor level, with walls terminated by a railing of pointed cusped arches supported on columns with capitals.

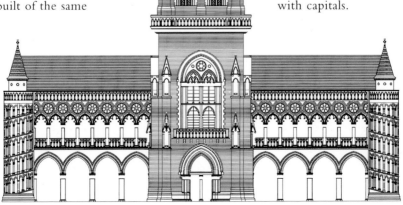

Montage of images from the University Buildings (clockwise from top): gargoyles adorning the Convocation Hall; Rajabai Tower; Homer looking down from a capital in the Library; 'caste' sculpture on the Convocation Hall; stone sculpture of Shakespeare on a capital in the Library; the entrance arch to the Library. Decorative stone foliage in the Convocation Hall (below).

Gargoyles protrude from the buttress, and the arcades double their divisions from the ground to the first floor. Above the second storey, small clerestory quatrefoil windows were let into the wall above a stringcourse of Porbandar stone adorned with more gargoyles. The façades were capped with parapet forms in an Early English bar-tracery pattern, feather-cut Porbandar stone roofs, four corner finials and a central attenuated parapet above the central peak of the roof. A bulging staircase was introduced on the northern end, and a recessed apse placed at the south. Windows provide ventilation at ground level, and are shielded by the groin-vaulted verandas of the first floor. Unlike the library, the Convocation Hall's verandas avoided the use of octagonal ribs.

Inside, the ceiling was composed of teakwood trusses, rafters and planking over a stone arched interior. Molecey proposed that the ceiling be painted in rust with gold highlights, the ornamental details being carried out to GG Scott's specifications.

Sir CJ Readymoney, the Convocation Hall's donor (top). *Engraving of GG Scott's Sir CJ Readymoney Convocation Hall* (below). *Aerial view of Convocation Hall from clock tower* (facing page).

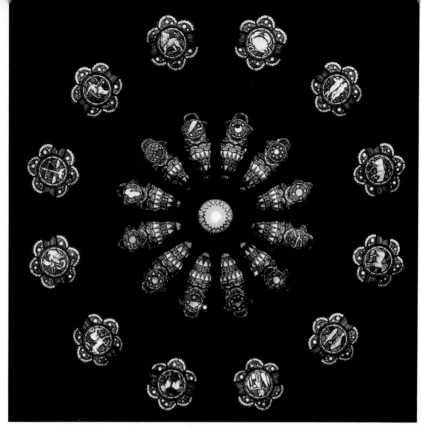

Rose window with zodiacal signs in its outer circle and the months of the year on its inner wheel.

A circular rose window with twelve divisions and a diameter of 20 feet pierces the northern façade. Its stained glass depicts the months of the year, with the signs of the zodiac represented on the outer ring. The coats of arms of Sir Bartle Frere, Sir Seymour Fitzgerald, Sir Philip Wodehouse, and Sir George Russell Clerk, successive governors of Bombay, can be seen in the eastern lancet lights. The rose, the shamrock and the thistle symbolize England, Ireland and Scotland in the stained glass below. Sir Cowasjee Jehangier's coat of arms, and those of England, Scotland, Ireland, Wales and Bombay are depicted in the western stained glass windows. Molecey designed the iron brackets supporting the gallery below, which were originally painted blue and gold. They rest on corbelled heads, each of which represents one of the 'castes' of India. Above the gallery are sixteen pedestals made of red and white stone with Porbandar stone carvings and ornamental canopies. These were to house sculptures of eminent personages, but lie empty even today. The apsidal end is attached to the larger hall by an unornamented semicircular arch filled with a set of stained glass lancet windows by Heaton, Butler & Bayne.

The university complex took eight to twelve years to design and complete, and the buildings established new standards of proficiency in the city's architectural profession. Indian craftsmen cooperated on the sculptural scheme. Muccoond Ramchander, in particular, is credited with overseeing the stone carving, helped by Kipling and his students at the JJ School of Art. The school's trained artists responded to complicated and demanding commissions with work that significantly enhanced the appearance of the city's buildings, of which the university buildings are excellent examples.

The British congratulated themselves on getting Indian craftsmen, with their three thousand-year history of superb stone carving, to successfully understand the new style required by European Gothic architecture. Ramchander's delicacy of style won him several government commissions, and so widespread was his work in the 1870s and 1880s that he was appointed temporary executive engineer (4th grade) by the PWD. Quoting lower prices, he was able to undercut Kipling to gain the commission for carving the capitals in Byculla's Elphinstone College. He also devised 40 varieties of capitals for the apse of St Thomas's Cathedral.

The Times of India reported in 1874, "Native workmen have been as apt to learn as their confreres in Europe, and that architecture has now for the first time since the decadence of Mussulman art, a glorious future before her in India. Art can only be permanent when the knowledge of it has become indigenous, and this period in architecture is arriving – to a certain extent has already arrived – in India, for not only the carvings but the clay models necessary for them are wrought out by natives and some of them moreover, show a considerable aptitude for general design."

Convocation Hall interior with rib vaulting (right). *Carved Seoni sandstone capital* (top).

HIGH COURT

The High Court's bulk makes it the most prominent feature on the skyline seen from the Oval, and it was also the most expensive structure to build. Fuller, a self-professed specialist in the Early English style, submitted designs in 1870, while on furlough in London. Construction began on 1 April 1871, the wings commenced in 1872 and the building was completed in 1878. The prophecy that Fuller's design, incorporating features from drawings submitted earlier by Trubshawe, Paris and Molecey, would "undoubtedly be one of the most striking ornaments of this City" was proved correct.

The High Court has six storeys, a length of 562 feet and an overall height of 174 feet, and it is entirely surrounded by arcaded corridors. A large internal, centrally placed and top-lit staircase was provided in the plan. The main entrance with a *porte-cochère* faces west, and from there a corridor leads to the principal staircase, an entrance now used exclusively

High Court from Oval Maidan; note central tower with Venetian style projecting balcony and conical roofs capped by Justice and Mercy (below). General John Augustus Fuller (top).

by judges. The public gain access from the eastern side, through an entrance also connected to the central stairwell. A series of subsidiary circular staircases, on the western front of the central block and at the north and south ends of its arcaded corridors, was provided to enable vertical movement without a mandatory return to the centre. The staircases are all capped with conical roofs. The two central roofs hold aloft sculptures symbolic of 'justice' and 'mercy', and the end roofs are topped by finials. The central tower terminates in a massive, steeply sloped roof penetrated by a series of dormer windows and a grouping of four cupola forms at its corners, all originally capped by decorative metal cresting.

The plan provided several large courtrooms, divided on each floor as to function. Appellate and original courts were planned on the first and second floors, those for criminal proceedings on the others. The finest courtroom is located on the fourth and fifth floors of the central tower. Top-lit from lancet windows set into the sixth storey on all four sides, the flooring was of paved mosaic, and a teakwood gallery was provided for the public. This court is connected to the judges' corridor on the west. The public is separated from the main offices and official access routes on every level. A library is accommodated on the third floor over the western entrance. A spacious Venetian balcony, leading off this library, once commanded views of the sea beyond the Oval Maidan.

Fuller's use of exaggerated massing in the muscular neo-Gothic style humbles judge, jury and accused alike, asserting the importance of government, law and the judicial process. The sculptural programme within the building

Figures of Justice (top) and Mercy (right) on High Court roofs.

Venetian style balcony of the High Court's library.

matches this didactic theme. Gremlins and grotesques, borrowed from medieval ecclesiastical buildings, represent temptations encountered in the world outside the court. The corridor capitals are carved with birds, beasts, and symbolic representations of people displaying varying nuances of dress and gesture. GG Scott's work next door presumably inspired the polychromatic Venetian features and rich sculptural decoration on the arcades and balconies.

The High Court was planned as a highly serviceable structure, and the original PWD-designed neo-Gothic furniture and fittings are still in use. An eastern extension, constructed in 1909, cramps the original site but has left the western façade undisturbed, and fortunately, is sympathetic in style and use of materials.

PUBLIC WORKS DEPARTMENT OFFICE

Around the corner from the High Court, on Veer Nariman Road (earlier known as Church Gate Street), is the PWD office, the second building in Bombay to be designed by Wilkins. The architect, although on furlough in Europe while preparing his drawings, was sensitive to the presence of the General Post Office directly opposite the site. The PWD building harmonized with its neighbour in style, size and materials used.

Wassoodeo Bapoojee provided immediate supervision during the construction years, from 1869 to 1872, and probably also oversaw the sculptural details. Cost was a consideration for the government, and so blue basalt double facing with Kurla quoins was substituted for a facing of Kurla hewn stone, and the office space was increased.

Built on an east-west axis, the building's main façade faces north, not the preferred orientation for ventilation. The front elevation uses two devices to add visual interest: variation of the arch and pier openings on the east and west corner blocks in a four, three, six rhythm, starting from the ground; and a Venetian balcony at the third storey on the central tower, to echo and balance the protrusion of the ground floor's *porte-cochère*, at the north façade's centre. The tower encloses the interior's top-lit central staircase hall, and two small turret forms capped by cast iron finials mark the feature externally. In a feature similar to the High Court, subsidiary entrances and staircases at the rear of the building in the east and west blocks, provide freedom of movement in the building without the necessity of returning to the centre.

Many alterations were made to the original design, but the government ensured, at Wilkins's request, that the building retained the polychromatic Venetian Gothic style of the Secretariat. However, the PWD office is a more powerful, varied and, ultimately, finer composition than the architect's earlier endeavour. The subdivisions within the building have been better expressed, the façade is a more balanced and stronger whole, and the scale better understood. An annexe on the southwest corner of the building was completed in sympathy with the rest of the building in June 1895.

Engraving of Wilkins's PWD building showing north façade, with Venetian style arcades and details.

GENERAL POST OFFICE

Across the street from the PWD building is the former General Post Office. Begun in 1869 and completed in 1872, today it serves as the Central Telegraph Office. The second building to be completed in Frere's scheme for the Esplanade, its design was generated from several architect's plans. A plaque in the building designates Trubshawe and Paris as its architects, but its construction and design history is in fact more complex.

TR Smith first took credit for the design, but stated that he only "aided" the process. This would have been at the end of 1864, when he was in Bombay, and no later than mid-1865. The principal feature of his design was a flexible plan enabling additions to the structure to be carried out easily. It is also most likely that Smith's assistance was utilized for the scheme devised and submitted by Trubshawe. Then the chief architect of the Ramparts Removal Committee, Trubshawe left Bombay in 1866, overburdened by work and under a cloud of suspicion resulting from difficulties with his projects. He never returned to India, nor does he seem to have continued his practice in Britain.

The Smith-Trubshawe collaborative scheme does not exist in any published records, but the basic floor plan should be attributed to them. Paris stated that he adapted their design through the addition of a third storey. Several other changes took place on the first plan to meet the expanded needs placed on the building and to economize on overall costs, as Trubshawe's designs, sent from Britain, were too expensive. So, Trubshawe's towers were shortened, the postmaster general's residence was abandoned, simpler mouldings and sculptural details were adopted, and Ransome's Patent Stone, more economical than carved stone, was employed for the quoining and decorative details.

Murzban was the project's assistant engineer, and the

Paris's General Post Office under construction, c 1872.

building represents a career landmark for him as the earliest assignment to record his involvement. He is said to have discovered and replaced weak columns during the building's construction and was soon rewarded with a promotion. The Post Office design used Porbandar and Kurla stone facings, with blue basalt rubble infill. Minton tiles paved the floors, and Broomhall tiles with teakwood supports were used for the roof, all materials similar to those of other neo-Gothic buildings in Frere Town. Terracotta Broomhall tiles were preferred to slate and zinc, as they were cooler and crows could not easily displace these tiles.

Eaves with prominent brackets on the GPO.

Using an east-west axis, the principal façade of the building faces south. The three-storey structure reveals no protruding balcony forms, although arcades form part of the design. The *porte-cochère* is unusual as it has two storeys and a roofed terrace. The airy arcade, open on three sides, provided a comfortable tiffin (or lunch) room for postal clerks. The fourth side led to a public hall of two-storey height provided with a gallery. This cleverly conceived floor plan enabled air to circulate throughout the central block of the building, before the introduction of electricity for fans or air-conditioning. However, the atrium was replaced, at an unknown date, by a first floor to provide more office space. Unique to this building are large overhanging eaves on the second floor. Their wooden brackets form an attractive break between the roof and the main block below, and their generous shadows effectively cool the external walls, as a *chhajja* does.

It is difficult to determine how much of this detailing can be attributed to Smith and Trubshawe, but the innovative aspects of the first two levels make a strong case for their guiding hand. The layout of Paris's second floor is quite typical in comparison. Its "harmony of proportion" earned the General Post Office (GPO) high praise at the time. The "careful delicacy of the elaborate ornamentation" on its façade can be credited to Paris who had made a study of medieval sculptural forms.

DAVID SASSOON LIBRARY AND READING ROOM

The present site of the David Sassoon Library and Reading Room has an excellent position in the Frere Town development. Leased from the government for 999 years at a very reasonable rent, the institution sprang from an earlier Mechanics' Institute. Originally its library had "a museum of models, architectural designs, patents and other matters dealing with engineering and mechanical science" used principally by a group of foreign mechanics working at the mint and the government dockyard. The members had met in rented accommodation until David Sassoon's bequest of Rs 60,000 in October 1863.

Fuller designed the new building, based upon two documented proposals by John Campbell representing the firm of Scott & McClelland. While laying the foundation stone in 1867, Frere named the building the Sassoon Mechanics' Institute. The clock tower that finishes the building presently seen was completed in 1873. Murzban was Fuller's

assistant and he is credited with designing the furniture, metal brackets, floor tile patterns, bookshelves and stone sculptural details, although Kipling may have made a few models for the project. Minton tiles for the flooring and Taylor tiles for the roof were supplied from Britain. A trust endowed on David Sassoon's death provided Rs 20,000 to pay for Thomas Woolner's 'portrait statue' of the benefactor.

Polychrome stone entrance arch of Sassoon Library (left). Sculpture of the benefactor, David Sassoon (top).

The structure, renovated in 1997 for the first time in over a hundred years, remains largely unaltered. Fuller chose uniquely to employ Kurla rubble with contrasting coloured pointing as a facing material, thus achieving inexpensively a relatively flat surface with an enormous amount of irregular pattern variation and no horizontal emphasis. The delicacy of scale and the playful polychromatic decoration in Porbandar and Vasai sandstone contrast with the rugged masculine exterior surface to create a most effective design and one of the most idiosyncratic buildings in Frere Town.

Main front of library (right). *Reading room with Minton tile floor, teakwood spiral stair* (below).

Beyond the Fort Precinct

The architectural prescription Frere devised for Bombay naturally extended beyond the immediate Fort area. The style and structure of such buildings also form a part of his achievement, and the construction and design work were still in the hands of a select group of trained architects and engineers who followed the precepts laid down by Frere and his trusted lieutenants.

COWASJEE JEHANGIER BUILDING FOR ELPHINSTONE COLLEGE, BYCULLA

The Elphinstone College, Byculla, was planned and built in the 1860s, opposite the Victoria Museum and Gardens (now known as the Bhau Daji Lad Museum and Zoo). It was named after Governor Mountstuart Elphinstone, the man who shaped the administrative framework of the Western Presidency during his term from1819 to 1827. Trubshawe made designs for the building in 1864, Frere laid the foundation stone in 1866, and the college opened in 1871. Paris and Molecey prepared the working details for the plans, and Indian sculptors on the site adapted Kipling's full-sized sculptural models for the foliated details. Fuller supervised the project, but he did not contribute to its design. The building is now utilized as a railway hospital.

Several unusual features combine with the building's traditional outer corridors, *porte-cochère*, and stone materials. The tower's exaggerated height dominates the southwestern skyline. The original proposal was to build it over a Moorish-style triple arch, but the doorway was simplified, strengthened and shortened when built. The tower's balconies of wood and stone were enlarged to transform them into very distinctive external features, the largest balcony appearing on the eastern façade. The timber was cut and pierced into varied and elaborate stencil forms, and the brackets that support the balconies form galleries that rise from the second storey of the tower to the fourth. Readymoney, who underwrote construction costs for the college building, had

Dramatic projecting tri-level wood and stone balcony of tower.

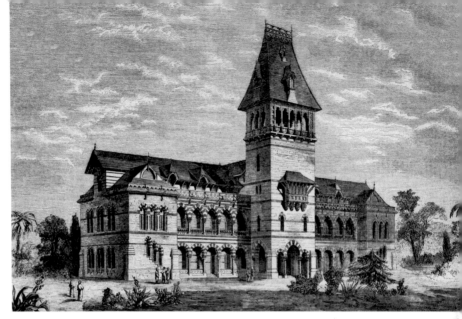

Engraving of Trubshawe's building for Elphinstone College, Byculla; note prominent central tower.

similar brackets on the façade of his house at Church Gate Street, a well-known example of this western Indian vernacular style in Bombay.

Another unusual feature of the building was the use of corrugated iron for the roof, presumably a cost-cutting measure, or perhaps a trial of this material. The front façade and basement also have long strips of coloured stone laid in courses of alternating colours. A basement was feasible here, although inadvisable in the Fort area, as Byculla, situated on higher ground, had low subsoil water levels. Four lecture halls occupied the ground floor and two fine large rooms flanked a small one on the first floor. A dormitory to accommodate 50 students was located on the third floor. The college's cast iron railings were shipped from Britain, and the original plans provided the garden with a small fountain. Intended as a prototype building of the 1860s, money and effort were lavished on its refinement and details. Although not as elaborate and expensive as GG Scott's university buildings, the Cowasjee Jehangier Building for Elphinstone College is one of the most singular and powerful compositions of the era. It is also more distinctively Indian in form than Scott's designs.

Neo-Gothic carved marble fountain in garden compound.

CRAWFORD MARKET

While providing designs for the Byculla college project, Kipling also worked extensively on sculptural plaques for the public entrance to the market named after the municipal commissioner, Arthur Travers Crawford. Still known familiarly as Crawford Market, the official name has now changed to honour Mahatma Jyotiba Phule.

Crawford, with Frere's support, was an energetic city planner during his term of office (1865-71). Capitalizing on the 1865 Municipal Act, and with the help of the legislative council, he prescribed zoning laws, adopted modern building practices and created a detailed health programme novel to Bombay. Crawford financed these undertakings with public monies and a rigid and thorough collection of taxes, which made him unpopular. As he also had a private interest in the Panwell Brick Kiln & Machine Co, that hoped to manufacture bricks for Bombay's public buildings, there was an organized public outcry, which contributed later to an incorrect assessment of his role in the written histories of the city's development. However, the market he promoted remains a notable success. The building was originally designed by Russell Aitken as a series of sheds for a piece goods bazaar, but a more extensive scheme was ultimately considered necessary.

Crawford arranged for a competition, advertised first in London, for market designs. William Emerson submitted the winning proposal, his being judged as most sensitive to the city's climatic conditions. Emerson may have drawn his entry *en route* to India to deliver Burges's proposal for the JJ School of Art, for he submitted it on arrival at Bombay in 1866.

Emerson's Crawford Market showing entrance with decorative tympanum overdoors and clock tower.

The flagship of several markets to be constructed, Crawford Market cost nearly ten times its lesser relations. In operation since 1871, its site, plan and design make it an excellent example of British architecture in Bombay.

Superbly sited near the railway station, between the Indian and the European areas of the city, the market was also at the intersection of two principal roads, and accessible to goods, traders and customers. Making the most of its corner location, Emerson constructed two long and low wings, 'ornamented sheds', that joined in a V-shape. At the apex, where the main streets converge, he placed a 128-foot high clock tower that could be widely seen. It advertised the market, adorned the cityscape and made an extremely effective focal point. To further enhance the corner profile, Emerson provided seven arched openings at street level, the entrances to the market, each with an elaborate wrought iron gate. Above three of the arched openings, tympanums, each with a sculptural

relief by JL Kipling, can still be admired by passers-by.

The plaque to the right of the central entrance depicts agriculture, and the processes involved in the growing and selling of vegetables. The plaque to the left illustrates the sale of fruit products in a generalized market scene. A central panel, between the two deeply carved fine Porbandar stone plaques, carries a dedication to Crawford with the date 1868.

The market wing on the left was designed for fruit and flowers and measures 150 by 100 feet, and the larger one on the right for vegetables

Kipling's deep relief figural plaques of 'market scene' (top) and 'agriculture' (centre). Crawford Market's commemorative tympanum with decorative carved side panels (bottom).

and spices measures 350 by 100 feet. The walls were finished in smooth Kurla stone, with wrought iron and cast iron adorning the sheds. Incorporated into the sheds' superstructure were cast iron lamp brackets. Emerson designed them as griffins to support lamp standards with their wings and twisted bodies. Their feet clutched at the column of a roof support, and each mouth firmly held another griffin whose neck and head transformed into a gas jet. Today, light sockets have replaced the gas jet fixtures. This type of ornamentation is reminiscent of Burges, but the master seldom used cast iron to such effect.

Russell Aitken designed the roofs of the market. Built on two levels they provide light and air efficiently to the sheds. Ventilators on top of their ridgepole increase the roof's cooling effect. Emerson paved the space with flagstone from Caithness, Scotland. A non-porous and tough stone, it was employed for its sanitary qualities and durable nature. This flagstone also contributes towards keeping the inner halls cool. For similar reasons, marble

was used for the display slabs in the meat and fish section. Sanitary conditions were also improved upon by the market's slaughtering procedures being defined and controlled by the municipality.

Emerson described the style of Crawford Market as 12th century French Gothic because he used features from this idiom: unglazed rose windows with complicated bar-tracery inserts and lion-head dripstones, which he tucked into the squinches of the Kurla stone arches of the side elevations. The windows were inserted at the end of the main market halls. The decorative outer shell provided the

Engraving of Emerson's market fountain (left).
Decorative cast iron griffin lamp bracket (top).

street with an ornamental and handsome building, while the interior was a highly practical market area.

Emerson also proposed a superintendent's house for the complex. Little is known of the intended design, except that it was to cost £16,000, too great an expense for the municipality, particularly after the financial crash in Bombay. The proposal incorporated a corner turret that was, in 1866, a precursor by nine years to a similar feature in Burges's own London home.

In 1874, an ornamental fountain was built at the northwest corner of the market courtyard, behind the main entrance. A watercolour design

Market fountain with carved alligators, dog and bear spouts, and reclining river goddess plaques.

for the fountain was displayed at the Royal Academy in 1870. The design source for Bombay's fountain derives directly from Burges's drawn fantasies for the Sabrina Fountain in Britain. Certain similarities of form are perceived in Emerson's choice of narrative symbols and in the intended site of his design. Furthermore, Emerson's drawings specified a four-tiered structure, with a bird standing on a ball at the top of the composition, above spouts formed from the upper bodies and mouths of bears. The bears were placed amongst a grouping of gable and pinnacle forms in which the rest of their bodies stood. At a lower level, sculptures of fish were portrayed on a bowl supported by a cluster of four columns. Level three of the fountain had alligator, ram and cow sculptures, as well as gargoyles. Below these, in a series of plaques carved by Kipling, were depicted four Indian river goddesses interspersed with the native birds of India. Standing in a larger pool was another set of four bigger plaques depicting figures performing a series of tasks, nestled between piers of coarse cut Porbandar stone. From here, ramps were to run out to more gargoyles and Gothic stanchions placed in the largest pool, an idea excluded from the final construction. Indian vegetable forms, reflecting wares sold in the market, profusely decorate the entire fountain. By and large, Emerson's original plan resembles the fountain as built.

The Crawford Market fountain was originally placed in a garden courtyard setting. That bucolic setting and a conveniently placed teashop used to provide a convivial meeting-ground for servants and traders alike. Emerson intended this small grouping to create a refreshing and calming centre in the busy market. Today, the garden around the fountain has disappeared to provide for temporary sheds and more shops, and the market is exceedingly busy. The future of the market fountain itself is also insecure. In 1985, the municipality covered it with a metal canopy, damaging its top, an action that gave official sanction to additional market stalls that obscured the fountain and filled in the open area around it. Its sculptures have been further damaged and painted, and without water, it is quite neglected and its future looks bleak.

The Crawford Market complex covers a total area of three acres. Boundary walls enclose the quadrangle at the back, pierced by gates that allow access to goods vehicles. Sheds abut these walls, constructed of smooth Kurla stone. Rienzi Giesman Walton made an addition to the market sheds, at an unknown date, but the original design was so well conceived that it is still used with little other alteration, and remains the finest market in the city. Thus, it is easy to understand how the whole complex, conceived as a superb ornament to the city, was described when it opened as "the noblest and most useful of all the public improvements executed in Bombay" and a monument to Crawford. The thriving market is still an attraction for visitors to the city.

Emerson's muscular Gothic fountain at Rusi Mehta Chowk, probably a rejected version for Crawford Market. Its central shaft bears allegorical armorials of three prominent British contributors to High Victorian Gothic Bombay: the artist JL Kipling (top), the urban planner AT Crawford (centre), and the architect W Emerson (bottom); their skills united to build a beautiful city.

EMERSON'S CHURCHES

French Gothic detailing appears on three churches designed by Emerson in Bombay, influenced undoubtedly by Burges who found the larger scale of the style both noble and economical. According to Burges, the "small pretty buildings" of medieval English architecture were unsuited to the "smoky atmosphere" of 19th century England. Burges's churches were more elaborately planned, but probably suggested design approaches for Emerson's early work in Bombay.

Emerson's clients needed a noble yet economic style as they all had restricted budgets and an austere vision of ecclesiastical spaces. Their buildings were required to convey "boldness, breadth, strength, sternness and virility" to convert non-Christians to the faith. All three churches were designed or built within a year and within a mile of each other in small rural communities. Girgaum was at the time still the 'hill village' and Khetwadi 'the place of fields'. Each church was designed in what can be perceived as a variation on a theme, their construction budgets and functional purposes being similar.

St Paul's Church, Kamathipura, was designed in 1866 and built in 1872 for a mere Rs 30,000. It has a rectangular nave, 46 feet long, 24 feet wide and about 100 feet high, with a chancel raised on a dais of three steps.

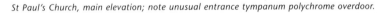

St Paul's Church, main elevation; note unusual entrance tympanum polychrome overdoor.

There is a centrally placed font, a series of double-height windows on the eight-bay long sidewalls, and round-arch windows above. A simple but massive rough cut stone façade employs a series of setback walls and two types of stone. Emerson enlivened the exterior with variations in the stone finishes, using pointed red Vasai stone infill for the arch over the door, and the same stone with a smooth edge above. These effects, combined with the use of teak doors, oversized blocks of stone in the entrances, and a pair of small pointed arches inserted into the entrance wall, successfully created an affordable but interesting façade. The entrance front remains unfinished, evidenced by brackets that protrude from the wall to support a structure planned for over the entrance porch but never carried out. However, sculptural features, the tympanum, gargoyles, and cast iron door hinges do give the church a dramatic impact. Emerson had also planned mural decorations of devotional subjects for the church's interior, but there is no evidence of these ever being completed. If carried out at all, they no longer exist. St Paul's style could be called 'minimal Early French', in the mode of a church constructed in 1863 by Burges in Brighton, and to which it relates in structural size and budget.

Emmanuel Mission Church with dramatic muscular Gothic tower and oversized rugged details.

The Emmanuel Mission Church, Girgaum (1867-69), with the Reverend TK Whitehead as patron, was built for the Church Missionary Society of Bombay. It is located near Grant Road, just east of the railway station. Opened on 10 January 1869, a watercolour drawing of its apse was exhibited at the Royal Academy the following year. An itinerant associate member of the RIBA reported in *The Times of India* that "a better bit I have seldom seen, never of its size, and peculiar treatment". He praised it for its perfection of detail and exquisite carving.

The original structure was erected for about Rs 45,000, but since then two transepts and a picturesque belfry have been added (1877), which cost Rs 16,000. Then, in 1885, a terraced *porte-cochère*

Frog gargoyle (top right), *carriage porch* (top left), *and nave* (right) *of Emmanuel Mission Church.*

Exceptional Saunders & Co stained glass lancet window.

was added at the south entrance, and CEG Crawford, as a memorial to his wife, placed an organ chamber at the south side of the western transept. The details added to the church since it opened conform to the spirit of Emerson's original designs. The church is orientated on an unusual north-south axis and it possesses a spectacular total immersion bath and a baptismal font in its southwestern porch. The Emmanuel Church was larger than St Paul's, Kamathipura, and more than one-third as costly to build. It could seat 300 people. Emerson, who was always proud of his design for this church, made a personal gift of the Minton floor tiles in 1869.

The church was built with roughly finished weather-resistant and muscular Kurla rubble laid in courses, with both rough and smooth finished Porbandar stone dressings. A modified teak kingpost roof on the interior supported an external corrugated iron roof. Emerson achieved distinctive and impressive quoined effects with Porbandar stone around the windows and doors. Floriated capitals were to be seen on the exterior columns of the *porte-cochère*, which was composed of four clustered colonnettes. Two magnificent frog gargoyles are now in a sad state of neglect. The church interior also has floriated capitals with coloured marble columns, some now painted white, stained glass window inserts in the cinquefoils above the nave's lancet windows, trefoil and round arched windows with a rose window placed in the south end of the nave, and comfortable benches. A series of fine memorials from the Victorian era are set into the walls. Kipling and his students are credited with the sculptural work. The stone carving inside and out is of the finest quality, and adds considerable interest to the building. MJ Higgins designed the ironwork, and Emerson collaborated with Saunders & Co to provide the four geometrical stained glass windows in the building's chancel, the only known examples of this exceptional company's work in India.

It was agreed at the time that the building was designed by a man with "a soul for his art" as it was pleasing in every respect. It is indeed a shame that the building is under threat of alteration and distortion. It has been used to buttress an apartment block built into the northwest wall of the apse and nave. In addition, the stonework suffers from serious decay while buildings and vegetation encroach upon the churchyard.

The Ambroli Mission Church, Khetwadi (1867-69), or the Free Church Mission, opened on 12 October 1869. A committee headed by Dr John Wilson (in whose honour Wilson College, Chowpatty, is named) approved Emerson's church, which seats 500 people and cost Rs 30,000 to build. Only "the proposed extensions at the eastern end [were] to be considered unnecessary."

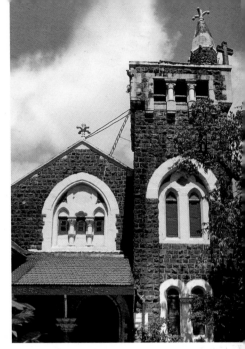

Emerson's Ambroli Church entrance front.

The Ambroli Church faces east, has a length of five bays and was constructed of Kurla stone with Porbandar stone detailing. Lancet windows with Porbandar stone surrounds were used as fenestration, inserted into pointed arch openings to create a strong geometric pattern.

The spare church interior had a simple hammerbeam roof with teakwood supports. There was a round arched apse at the eastern end of the church, within which the altar was raised on a dais. The rectangular nave had two enclosed rooms at the western end, on the left a vestry and on the right a staircase and base for the three-storey belfry tower. The belfry comprised a square room with a sloping roof, placed at 90 degrees to the main roof axis of the nave below. The room at the top of the tower was stepped out slightly from the façade, with bracket supports in Porbandar stone, and above the roof was a peculiarly shaped cap, also of Porbandar stone. The cap extends 30 feet above the roof, and terminates with a finial similar to the one atop the main crest of the nave's roof.

The church has a very rugged and asymmetrical appearance, as the tower distorts the balance of the composition. Perhaps Emerson's plans for the eastern end of the church would have modulated this effect. An apartment block for the 'native ministry' was erected at the western corner of the garden, almost adjoining the main body of the church and considerably disfiguring Emerson's building.

DAVID SASSOON BUILDING FOR ELPHINSTONE HIGH SCHOOL

Adjacent to the Azad Maidan, on Mahapalika Marg (the former Cruikshank Road), stands the David Sassoon Building for the Elphinstone High School. This was Molecey's most unusual but finest work in Bombay. Its foundation stone was laid in 1872, construction began in 1873, and Sir Albert Sassoon, First Baronet of Kensington Gore and eldest son of David Sassoon, contributed the entire cost. The school opened in 1879.

A proposal for the Cathedral High School by Paris and Molecey may have been the source for this plan. Designed in a most vigorous 'muscular'

Gothic style, the four-storeyed building faces south over the Azad Maidan. Its large and exceptionally broad staircase on the entrance front extends inexplicably to the first floor, and unusual dome-shaped turrets terminate its fourth storey, at either ends of this main elevation.

The school's ground and first floors are barrel vaulted, while those above are composed of wooden floors supported on stone brackets visible in the walls. The plan of the ground floor gives it the feel of a basement,

1890s' view of main front; note prominent turrets, central staircase and muscular Gothic forms.

as it is not raised on a plinth and is quite dark. Originally, the centre of the ground floor served as a playground, its cool properties being desired in the initial design. Over the playground, at the school's centre, was located the most spacious lecture hall, marked by a large gable designed by Molecey. Though the elevations appear symmetrical from the south, the school's central section is deeper than its two flanking wings. The wings contain classrooms, 32 in all, four masters' rooms, and arcaded corridors on the southern side.

The High School is built of rough cut Kurla stone with Minton tile floors and a Mangalore tile roof. Still to be seen is some fine wrought iron work and the excellent sculptural details on the building's exterior. The attentive observer will also find the massing of the structure captivating, as it is unusual and intentionally awkward.

Eight-sided turret with griffins, finial and wrought iron top.

CHIEF PRESIDENCY MAGISTRATE'S COURT

The Chief Presidency Magistrate's Court, or Police Court, on Cruikshank Road, was designed by Adams and opened in 1889. Adams also designed furniture for the interior. Murzban supervised the building's construction, and the JJ School of Art probably supplied the fine sculptural decoration of unusual placement and originality. The court has a striking appearance and its excellent design, massing and superb craftsmanship make it one of Bombay's finer constructions.

Disposed on an east-west axis with arcades surrounding the entire façade, the building accommodates courtrooms on the ground and first floors as well as administrative offices for the police and magistrates. A large enclosed staircase tower, at the east corner, is accentuated on the main elevation by a round turret form and long vertical lines of lancet windows pushing out over its entrance door. A finial, now removed, and crocketing were added to its roof. Its three-storey high lancet windows enable the unusually handsome free-standing cast iron staircase to be naturally lit right to the top of the building. At the centre of the main elevation is a *porte-cochère* with the three-storey block built directly over it. The combination of these various unusual elements make for a most pleasing and satisfactory design.

Rooms were provided on the ground floor for messengers, water, records, stolen property and European constables, and also for a series of 'lock ups'. Barristers and solicitors, clerks, and the Third Presidency Magistrate's court was accommodated on the first floor, and on this floor were also waiting rooms for witnesses and prisoners' staircases. The second floor was similarly planned, but the courtroom on this floor was for the Chief Presidency Magistrate. A staircase led to the third floor where the chief constable's quarters comprised a living room, two bedrooms, two bathrooms and a cook's room, attached by a terraced roof.

Magistrate's Court from Azad Maidan (right).
Fine carved decorative stonework on main elevation (facing page).

A pair of griffins, serving as dripstones at the third floor level, and a massive round balcony at ground floor level adorn the main façade. Formed from a massive base appended to the wall, the balcony affords a view of the garden and is accessible from the first floor. Griffin forms on the main elevation were sculpted with extended wings and seem ready to leap off the structure – an amazing detail. A *flèche* attached to the roof further enlivens the building, as do panels of pierced wooden *jali* work, which help provide ventilation. Adams also used coloured stone inserts to spell out the building's function, on the third storey of the main elevation. Other decorative features include finial caps on gables with rose window

Rear view of Magistrate's Court, c 1900; note decorative flèche.

centres at the level of the roofline, and multifoil tracery windows inserted above smaller lancet-shaped openings in the arcades. A façade of consistent and balanced form was successfully avoided by articulating, in different ways, each area of its external plane.

The style of the building is Venetian Gothic with some French influence evident in the eastern entrance stairway, and in the *flèche* attached to the roof. Adams described the style simply as "medieval Gothic". Although extremely rich and decorative, the Magistrate's Court bears none of the iconographic complexity of the High Court. However, the quality of the capitals and woodwork compares favourably with the Victoria Terminus, completed in 1888 to FW Stevens's design.

The structure was considerably disfigured in 1983 with the addition of an elevator shaft, crudely built, on the main southern elevation. The *flèche* has suffered similar maltreatment by painting and panelling over its ventilation louvres. However, the rest of the building is in good condition, despite yellow paint applied most heavily to the exterior to match the painted woodwork but hiding, in the process, the fine sculptural details.

CLIMAX OF BOMBAY GOTHIC

FREDERICK WILLIAM STEVENS

FREDERICK WILLIAM STEVENS (1848-1900) is Bombay's most spectacular neo-Gothic practitioner, and he dominates the stylistic appearance of the city. Having collaborated on proposals for several large buildings undertaken by the Ramparts Removal Committee, he was familiar with the pitfalls and procedures of construction work in Bombay. The publicity gained from winning various architectural competitions undoubtedly led to his first important commission, the Royal Alfred Sailors' Home. Stevens was born in 1848 at Bath, Somerset, where he trained with a local architect. In 1867, he arrived in India, and began work at Bombay in 1869 after a two-year posting at Poona (Pune). Assigned to assist Paris, he was involved with the preparation of designs for the new European General Hospital, the revised design for the new General Post Office, the design for the new Telegraph Office (now demolished), and the Telegraph Signaller's Quarters.

FW Stevens (1848-1900), the foremost High Victorian Gothic Revival architect of Bombay.

In 1877 Stevens submitted a design, with Adams, for a college at Lucknow in northern India. It called for a large entrance porch, arcades built of horseshoe and pointed Indo-Saracenic arches in alternation, and brick and stone voussoirs. A small corbelled balcony was included, and the entrance sported circular turrets, capped with domes. Octagonal domes, covered with coloured 'Mooltan' tiles in a reticulated pattern, crowned its wings. The highest dome, resting on a pierced drum, surmounted the octagonal examination hall. Angle turrets with cupolas accentuated the main angles of the structure. This college proposal reveals direct parallels to later buildings designed by Stevens, and its design contributed to his evolution as an architect.

Bedford Lemere's 1890s' view (below) of GG Scott's
St Pancras Station, London (1868-74). Note long
train shed at left, pinnacled tower at centre with
porte-cochère entrance below, and distant clock
tower at right of entrance front. Deen Dayal's
1890s' view (facing pages) of Victoria Terminus
(1878-88); long train shed at left, pinnacled towers
with porte-cochère entrances below, left and right
of main entrance block.

VICTORIA TERMINUS

Stevens's various earlier projects enabled him to refine his architectural ideas. Ultimately, using that experience, he went on to construct one of the largest and most important buildings erected under European influence in the Indian empire. Iconic in character, for many people the station has become a visual symbol synonymous with Bombay itself. Stevens's most significant architectural work, it is the pre-eminent railway station of the Orient.

The railways in India were symbols of engineering prowess. They answered the challenge posed by vast inaccessible regions within the subcontinent with an order and structure worthy of the British empire. An engineering solution to the daunting task of connecting the disparate and distant sections of India, they forged the economic dominance of Bombay, and of the British as well. In addition, it miraculously linked all of India through the Suez Canal, another marvel of engineering, to the ports of Europe. This achievement – a truly extraordinary 19th century change to the world – parallels the internet of our time by its radical ability to connect people across continents and cultures.

The Victoria Terminus (VT) was built as offices and a terminal for the Great Indian Peninsula Railway, and is now officially called Chhatrapati Shivaji Terminus (CST). Conceived between 1876 and 1878, Axel Herman Haig drew the most elaborate perspective of the project in the

Main and east elevations showing entrance court to offices and effective overall massing (below). *Watercolour perspective of VT by Haig, Burges's principal draughtsman* (following pages).

Dome of VT with Progress *atop; note projecting gargoyles.*

latter year. Haig was a brilliant draughtsman and his watercolour helped to 'sell' Stevens's project. As Haig was also the draughtsman most frequently used by Burges, Stevens had to have been aware of Burges's work. At the time of its construction VT received tremendous critical acclaim and, prior to that, its plans were exhibited in 1879 in Bombay – where it won a gold medal – and at London's Royal Academy in 1880. Some of the hallmarks of Stevens's style, his particular fondness for domed structures, angle turrets and cupolas, are readily apparent in both Haig's perspective and in the final building.

Stevens's adaptation of the large dome to a secular neo-Gothic building is a novelty of formal massing that adds interest to an already fascinating construction. The station's octagonal dome was placed directly over the entrance hall, and the cantilevered staircase within leads to the company offices above. A dome was employed here merely for the dramatic effect it has on the cityscape and on the occupants of the building; it serves no other purpose. Stevens had mastered the challenge of building such a solid masonry construction on a neo-Gothic building without centring, and through the use of a new technique of dovetailed ribs created yet another novelty in design. In addition, the building's significant relationship to its host city is again reasserted, a kind of capitol building for a mercantile empire.

Upon receiving the commission for VT in 1878, Stevens left for Europe, on a ten-month furlough, to study other important railway termini. GG Scott's St Pancras Station (1868–74), only just completed in London, was clearly an important design source for him.

GG Scott's proposed designs for Berlin's Houses of Parliament had also only been published four years prior to Stevens's first proposals, and they too bear strong similarities to his completed station. Common features from this proposal include office wings that run at right angles to the main block, a central dome topped by an allegorical figure, and three entrance doors and gables at ground level, surmounted by a set of three bays of lancet windows with a rose window above.

That it took ten years to construct VT helps to indicate the vastness of the undertaking. When finished in 1888, the total expenditure was approximately £260,000, the highest for any building of that era in Bombay. Stevens closely supervised the project, although Siteram Khanderao was the PWD's assistant engineer and Mahderao Janardhan was the PWD supervisor.

Initially a station exclusively utilized by long-haul trains travelling to the interior of the subcontinent, today the station also services 2.5 million daily commuters. Despite that change, VT remains a symbol of civic pride, and it continues to vividly recall the railways' historic dominance of Bombay's fortunes. The structure's main façade is approximately 330 feet

Earp's allegorical sculpture of Progress atop VT's dome with crocketing and decorative finials below.

in height. Train sheds and platform bays extend another 1,200 feet from the main block. There is ample provision for light and air throughout the building, and great care was taken to protect offices and platforms from the sun's heat. The internal structural needs of this stone building are architecturally expressed in massive unadorned load-bearing masonry pylons, arches and piers. This traditional but expensive building technique is plainly evident in a series of exposed supports in the booking hall and along the offices.

Stevens's design for VT also made excellent use of its commodious site at the intersection of four major roads. Facing almost due west, VT has most of the concentrated centre of the city of Bombay in front of it, with the busy docks and the harbour behind. The wholesale Crawford Market and several residential areas are nearby. The site has remained a pivot for the city's commercial, official, educational and judicial life.

Stevens planned a garden in the forecourt, and a series of four beds to the rear, which have now given way to built structures. A mound with a central fountain lends emphasis to the front garden, around which a drive leads to the central block's *porte-cochère*, and the main entrance staircase. The forecourt garden is visible from the office corridors, and provides a softening touch to the elaborate 'muscular' forms of the building massed around it. With the same purpose in mind, Stevens provided a garden at the rear, enclosed by wings comprising the lavatory for travelling gentlemen, the staff kitchens, a corridor and the waiting hall adjacent to the stationmaster's office. This northern flank of the building remains open to the public, and here a carriage porch gives access to a groin-vaulted entrance hall that serves as the booking office.

The interior of the booking hall is lavishly treated with groining in the ceiling, originally painted blue, gold and strong red on a ground of rich blue with gold stars. The walls were lined with glazed tiles, all made by Maw & Co of Britain, and a dado rail of foliated design in red and buff colours on a dark base of chocolate, buff and black were included in the design. Above the dado, the walls were lined

Gothic groin-vaulted two-aisle interior of VT's booking hall. Note balcony at left.

Decorative wrought iron capital of train shed.

with white Porbandar stone. The floors were paved with unglazed coloured tiles arranged in large panels of geometrical and foliated designs. The tympanums of the windows were filled in with panels of coloured glass of varied designs and subdued tints, the latter having the effect of toning down the glare of the Indian sun, and serving to throw a soft and cool light over the hall. The counters, now extensively remodelled, had brass railings, and were executed in local woods of different colours by the East India Art Manufacturing Co. Around the hall, on the first floor, were placed corridors, or galleries, for use by the railway staff, and the arch openings were filled with wrought iron ornamental railings finished with French polished teakwood handrails. The railing was painted a chocolate brown and highlighted in bright red and gold. According to Stevens's instructions, the capitals for the booking hall were carved *in situ* out of a single piece of white Seoni sandstone. Red and grey Italian marbles for the column clusters supplemented the decorative effect. Yet other coloured marbles were used for the corridor details credited to the coloured stone contractor Gibello. The intent was to fashion a polychromatic space rich in sculptural detail and employing a variety of materials. Master sculptor Gomez and the students of the JJ School of Art under the direction of John Griffiths (1837–1918), Superintendent, designed the sculpture models. Guided by Europeans, Indian craftsmen skilfully executed the metal and stone decorative scheme.

Added to this, and reaffirming the Gothic design intent, was a series of decorative tympanums, pediments and sculptures placed on the exterior. Thomas Earp, of the firm of Earp, Son & Hobbs, carried out this work in London in Bath stone. The following subjects were depicted at the apex of the pediments: *Commerce*, on the southwest corner of the main façade, was depicted by a central figure expressing invitation and welcome, a figure on the left holding Britannia's trident, and another on the right holding a laurel wreath in her left hand to represent successful enterprise, a clipper

Engineering *atop pediment of northwest corner of main façade, with rose window below.*

ship symbolizing trade placed beneath her right hand; *Agriculture*, on the south façade, depicted by a central figure with a cornucopia and ploughshare symbolizing plenty, a figure on the left with a dibble and seeds for sowing, and a figure on the right with a sickle and sheath of wheat as a symbol of reaping; and *Engineering*, on the northwest corner of main façade, depicted by a central figure with the cylinder of a steam engine, a figure on the left with a gunner's quadrant (military engineering), and a figure on the right with a screw propeller (naval engineering). All of these sculptural groups is 10 feet high, 8 feet 6 inches wide, and each is composed of three blocks of stone. In addition, each was intended as the principal decorative element on its respective façade.

Entrance guardians to office block, a 'tiger of India' at right, a 'lion of Britain' at left.

In addition, *Progress* stands atop the central dome of the station, 14 feet in height. She carries a copper gilt flaming torch in her right hand, and her left hand holds a winged wheel which rests at her side. T Earp also depicted Queen Victoria beneath the central axis of the dome at the level of the second storey (now removed). She stood holding the orb and sceptre in her right and left hands beneath a canopy attached to the wall.

Tympanums at the ground floor level depict: *Science*, embodying astronomy, electricity, physical geography, medicine, chemistry, and mechanics, on the northwest *porte-cochère* main façade; and *Trade*, on the southwest *porte-cochère* main façade, represented by the central figure of peace fostering harmonious relations between east and west, peace being an essential condition of commerce.

In further elaboration of this decorative scheme, two feline creatures were placed at the gates to the main block, (one a lion to represent British interests in India, the other a tiger to represent the national symbol of India), side by side at the entrance and exit to the great office building.

There are also ten large bas-relief portrait roundels on the western façade. These depict the founders, directors, and important figures behind the railway's historic development. Eight of these are placed at ground level, in the space above the squinch area in the arcade of the central block's courtyard. The men are (according to the original spellings as seen on reliefs): on the left, Sir J Jijibhai Bart, Lord Reay, and Lord Elphinstone; on the *porte-cochère*, the Earl of Dufferin, and the Marquess of

Dalhousie; on the right, Mountstuart Elphinstone, Sir Bartle Frere Bart, and J Shunkersett. There are two more portrait roundels above this, on the first floor level, depicting Watt and Colonel Holland. Another set of portrait roundels on the southern façade, of the same size, includes one of James J Berkeley, the engineer who masterminded many of the railway's difficult building schemes. On a smaller scale, the 'castes' of India are represented in sixteen bas-relief heads in each corner drum of the main façade's inner courtyard, at the north and the south. Added to this, peacocks, egrets, lotus flowers, monkeys and coats of arms are depicted in sculptural relief on tympanums throughout the public spaces and entrances to the building.

The style chosen to accommodate such an ornate decorative scheme was modified Italian Gothic. Oriel forms, crocketing, arches with and without cusping, single and clustered columns, buttresses and battered setbacks, gargoyles and griffins abound on the surface. Despite a seemingly symmetrical floor plan, variations in window openings and arch rhythms were incorporated to suit the requirements of ventilation and shade. For those interested, this building can be studied on the scale model displayed in the main staircase entrance hall.

Ram's head gargoyle (below left), *and a cartouche* (below right) *with the GIP railway coat of arms borne by a lion, between crocketing and a dog gargoyle.*

Montage of details from Victoria Terminus (clockwise from left): portrait roundels of Watt and Colonel Holland above the GIP Railway crest; an allegorical representation of India, the peacock decorates a tympanum; figures in a sculptural group framed by crocketing on a ground-floor pediment; details of corner drum on the railway administration building; details of capitals depicting Indian animals and foliage – a cobra and mongoose in confrontation flanked by a pair of owls; a pangolin and a parrot; a leaping griffin and a cat with a mouse in its mouth in deep relief at the crotch of joined gables.

ROYAL ALFRED SAILORS' HOME

The Royal Alfred Sailors' Home (now the Maharashtra State Police Headquarters), took four years to construct. Completed in 1876, it stands at the corner of Frere Road and Colaba Causeway (both now parts of Shahid Bhagat Singh Marg). The Sailors' Home's outstanding architectural qualities brought in many more assignments for Stevens, including his most famous, the Victoria Terminus. The first floor originally provided sleeping accommodation for 20 officers and 38 sailors, while the second floor slept another 20 sailors, a total of 78 seamen. Stevens's project in the 'domestic' Gothic style was quite luxurious in its heyday, boasting wide corridors, airy rooms and luxurious bathrooms.

The central gable bears a relief sculpture by Richard Lockwood Boulton depicting Neptune surrounded by nymphs and sea horses in a triangular-shaped pediment with crocketing above. To the left and right, two griffins bear shields that display coats of arms. Kipling designed these figures and other decorative exterior sculpture, including the circular marble bas-relief of Baroda's Gaekwad Sayaji Rao II on the entrance porch. Burjorjie Nowrojie of the JJ School of Art designed the highly ornamental ironwork, the staircase railing, and the iron finials and castings. J Macfarlane & Co of Glasgow built the exceptional iron gates in the entrance hall and iron grilles installed in the ground floor arch openings.

Stevens's Sailors' Home; note projecting eaves with prominent brackets and central raised pediment.

Boulton's deep relief plaque showing Neptune with nymphs and sea horses, beneath crocket details.

Stevens made careful plans for the circulation of both people and air in the building. He designed a corridor 9 feet 6 inches deep that encased the structure, and two sets of stairs allowed the superintendent and his family privacy at their end of the building. There were arcades to provide cool and covered access to the lavatories, and these, for odour and health reasons, were placed at a sufficient distance from the sleeping quarters. A recreation ground, at the rear, could be seen from the corridors that doubled as verandas. This arrangement allowed residents to watch the progress of games or to 'take the air', all in cool shade and with a view of the harbour. A library and capacious baths were also incorporated.

The building, a massive Kurla stone masonry structure in the adapted neo-Gothic style of Bombay, is of great importance to understanding Stevens's later work. Its general massing, with a central block and the twin towers at each end of the main elevation, create a powerful design with a varied and attractive roofline. The corner towers probably owe their inspiration to Bombay's Telegraph and Post Offices by Paris, as Stevens had just finished work on these projects. In the Sailors' Home, the roofs flared outward on timber supports to create deep shade to the stonework below, as *chhajjas* do. Another feature worth noting in this building is the solid appearance and central placement of the main staircase. Round arches of blue basalt stone support the staircase, and its central placement recurs in most buildings designed by Stevens in Bombay.

Trubner & Co's carved wood balcony (1887), on 7 East 10th Street, New York.

BATTLE OF STYLES

Though Stevens's scheme for VT seems triumphant today, when it was built a battle of styles was brewing. The challenger was RF Chisholm, an architect who advocated the Indo-Saracenic style. Chisholm won a competition in 1883 to build offices for the Bombay Municipal Corporation (BMC) across the intersection from the terminus. However, in the end his challenge failed, and Stevens prevailed.

To explain further, the architectural style employed by Bombay until the 20th century was more closely coupled to Europe than to India. Although changing architectural attitudes in Britain were paralleled in India by the 1880s, Bombay was slow to change. Once the Gothic Revival style advocated by Frere was employed, it was the undisputed choice of architectural style for every large public commission. In the meantime, Kipling and Frederick Salmon Growse, a member of the Indian Civil Service, initiated an argument for the use of Indian design in objects and architecture executed on Indian soil. Started in 1885 by Lockwood de Forest, Trubner & Co simultaneously attempted to popularize Indian domestic architectural features in Europe and America, reinforcing currents of cross-cultural sharing prevalent in the era. The style of Chisholm's entry parallels loosely in time and method the same motivation to innovate in architectural approach as advocated by these other theorists. His revisionist approach reflected a reaction to an 'Englishness' of official attitudes in India that had begun to seem inappropriately chauvinistic around this time. The ensuing battle of styles even went on to develop political connotations towards the end of the century. In Bombay, however, the use of a particular style was perceived as merely an aesthetic choice. The historicism that motivated the study and reverence of ancient Indian forms was considered valid when applied to other styles as well, such as Venetian Gothic, which Bombayites preferred.

BOMBAY MUNICIPAL CORPORATION BUILDING

Soon after VT was completed in 1888, work began on new offices for the Municipal Authority to celebrate its promotion to corporation status. The project's design history elucidates the battle of styles confronting Bombay. For more than 20 years, the city fathers and benefactors perceived neo-Gothic as the only distinguished style in India. They also felt it had helped make Bombay architecturally unique in the subcontinent. So, although neo-Classicism had not prospered in Bombay, there was a real challenge to Gothic from the Indo-Saracenic style. Stevens appreciated this dilemma, and analysing the ground, he elected to amalgamate selected Hindu and Mughal elements into his admired Gothic designs. This was a gradual process, but a successful formula, and it guaranteed Stevens's architectural pre-eminence until his death. The building is the most explicit challenge to neo-Gothic's position, so the project is examined here in some detail.

The original designs for the municipal building were generated from an 1883 competition open to entrants from London. The V-shaped site was opposite VT, then only a work in progress. Chisholm won first prize with a design in the Indo-Saracenic style, and construction began the following

South elevation of BMC facing Cruikshank Road with floor plan (inset); note V-shape enclosing garden.

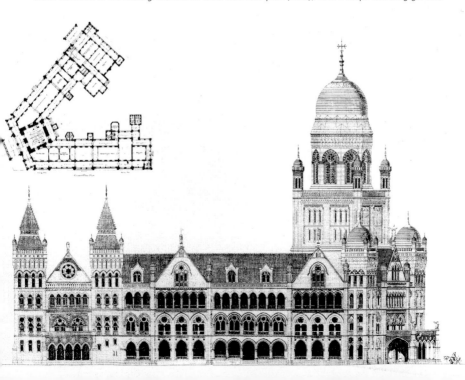

year. Soon work was stopped by government order, amid suggestions that Chisholm had underestimated building costs, but the official reason provided was that a change of site had been suggested. In fact, four alternative sites were evaluated, but Chisholm suspected that the real reason lay in the unpopularity of his 'Hindoo-Saracenic' style with the authorities.

Four years passed before the original site was once again preferred. Then, new designs for a more costly building, in keeping with the organization's new importance as a corporation, were requested from Chisholm. His revised proposal was also in the Indo-Saracenic style, as he had hoped that this commission would mark a turning point in his career. He believed that by affecting a change in the official architectural preferences of Bombay he would mark out a new city to build in, but he was refused the commission. Ultimately, his designs achieved success only in Madras (Chennai) and Baroda (Vadodara), and his only construction in Bombay was the Indo-Saracenic annexe on Apollo Pier Road (now Chhatrapati Shivaji Marg) to Watson's Hotel. The annexe was later demolished to make way for Dhanraj Mahal.

Chisholm's fierce defence of his position in *The Builder* of 1888 outlines his struggle. Ironically, it was he who nominated Stevens five years earlier to the RIBA, and as consulting architect to Gaekwad Sayaji Rao III of Baroda, Chisholm felt entitled to speak out candidly against his opponent.

Not only style, but also time was an enemy of Chisholm's proposal. For, when the keystone of VT's 45-foot wide dome was installed in July 1887, the press discussed and praised the finished structure at great length. So great was the response that Stevens retired from the PWD in 1888, to found his own firm. His withdrawal from public service enabled him to vie for the Bombay Muncipal Corporation commission, immediately putting Chisholm at a disadvantage. Adams, then the acting Architectural Executive Engineer, was a close friend of Stevens, and moreover, he opposed Chisholm's proposal on stylistic grounds. Adams and Stevens had worked jointly on various projects, such as the Government House at Malabar Point. Stevens was also on very friendly terms with Grattan Geary, president of the BMC, having designed Geary's private residence in Lonavala. However, the final outcome in this battle of styles was affected primarily by stylistic preferences, and Gothic won a few years reprieve.

In order to be awarded the BMC commission, Stevens promptly submitted designs when requested by the Corporation. The two coloured drawings, one of the exterior and the other showing the interior of the Council Chamber, made convincing arguments for his design. Before

BMC main entrance elevation with dome and flanking wings.

Section on line A.B.

making his proposal, Stevens had studied the new town halls of Europe. This helped him both to overcome the difficulties of his site and provide for a convenient and well-ventilated building for the municipality. Stevens described the style of his building as "a free treatment of early Gothic with an Oriental feeling, which, I consider, the best adapted for the site the buildings are to occupy." He diplomatically stated that because the style of Frere Town had been chosen "after careful deliberation and consultation with some of the most eminent architects in England and Bombay at that time" it was necessary to keep new structures compatible with this pattern.

When making his proposal it is clear that Stevens was aware of Chisholm's design, and Stevens's own design

Interior cross-section of entrance hall staircase and double dome above.

was similar in many ways. This is partly because the V-shaped site considerably reduced the design options, and Stevens's approach was calculated as a compromise between accepted styles and changing attitudes. The widespread support his plan and stylistic preference garnered can also be attributed to Stevens's good instinct for public relations. Capitalizing on his local knowledge and a good understanding of the city commissioners' predilections, he adopted a moderate stance on the mixing of styles. This assured a popular reception to his design, while it also wisely ensured that the impact of his neo-Gothic VT, opposite, was in no way reduced. In truth, by winning this commission, Stevens ensured that his two complementary edifices, each of which is far greater in scale than any of its neighbours, would dominate the entire square before them.

Work on the BMC building to Stevens's design commenced in 1889. His building employed the latest technology available, so that more than 20 years before electricity was introduced to the city at large, the BMC building was inaugurated fully electrified. Concrete floors were also used, making the

Allegorical figure of Urbs Prima in Indis, *astride India, and holding a ship aloft in her right hand.*

structure partially fireproof, and the building had the capacity to store 40,000 gallons (almost 182,000 litres) of water in tanks within the roof, to not only fight fires but also run the hydraulic lifts.

The final plan made excellent use of the oddly shaped site. Stevens converted the corner into the focal point of the design by erecting a tall façade capped by a dome, marking the intersection of the major roads. The two flanking façades, on Cruikshank and Hornby Roads, contributed balance and cohesion to the edifice. Stevens pushed his building up to the limits of the plot's boundaries, utilizing the space captured inside the V as a garden. He also made the BMC building 20 feet taller than VT, to ensure it was not overshadowed by its nearest neighbour. However, when viewed from the pavement in front of the building, the flat, gable-fronted façade, related to the human scale at street level, partially obscures the high dome above it, a comforting human touch, demonstrating Stevens's mastery of massing. To add further interest, atop the central gable, flanked by dome-capped towers, is a sculpture by the British artist Hems, representing *Urbs Prima in Indis*, the motto devised by Frere and adopted by the BMC. The overall composition of this main façade, adorned by an allegorical sculpture, harmonized well with its companion, the VT, although the minaret forms above and the outer bulbous dome were more Indian in appearance. However, multifoil windows, pointed arches and arcades all relied on Italian Gothic sources, not Indo-Saracenic ones.

Stevens placed the BMC's main entrance and *porte-cochère* at the elbow of the V, on the building's southeastern elevation. High above this was a records room, situated in a square space within the roof, below the uppermost water tanks but above an inner dome, visible only from inside the BMC entrance hall. The outer dome, which can be viewed only from the street, rises to 235 feet, more than double the height of the inner dome covering the staircase. Underneath this inner dome is the main staircase, which leads upward from the entrance's central hall. The entrance hall is a marvellous space, visually astonishing and a treat to the

Interior cross-section of Corporation Hall showing stained glass at left and visitors balcony, centre.

uninitiated, as Oriental elements were quite elaborately applied to its design. The richly finished interior of the central hall serves as an atrium with corridors on several levels, through which a grand staircase with marble treads rises for one of the three floors. The staircase then connects to arcaded corridors that wrap around the wide and open central core, connecting to both the lifts and the internal corridors of the offices. Capping the hall is its elaborately decorated dome, inspired by the Gol Gumbaz of Bijapur, according to Stevens. This inner dome is an erudite example of the architect's constructive skill. Its height of approximately 95 feet, within a space only 40 feet square, inspires both awe and surprise. To support the dome, Stevens's hall has granite colonnettes and arches on its four interior walls, from which fan vaults spring to support the circle of the lower inner dome that sits upon this base.

Within the BMC offices, the other outstanding space is the Corporation Hall. It has an interior of exceptionally handsome design, 65 feet long, 32 feet 6 inches wide, and 38 feet high. After an extensive fire, it was restored in 2000-01 by preservation architect Vikas Dilawari. At one end of the hall is a full height bay window decorated with coloured stained glass inserts. Before the bay window there used to stand a raised platform, to make speakers more visible and audible, an idea Stevens borrowed from the Birmingham Council Chamber. Stevens also supplied an external cast iron spiral stair, which leads to a visitors' gallery, a concept he borrowed from the Glasgow Municipal Building. (The Corporation Hall is now closed to the public.) To finish off the hall Stevens designed all its furniture and woodwork in blackwood and teak, and it was manufactured by Wimbridge & Co of Bombay to the highest quality. (Most of this furniture is now dispersed from the BMC collections.)

Opened in 1893, the BMC building offers practicality, considerable charm and comfort to its users. Added to the exteriors' embellishments were some beautiful pierced *jali*-work shades of sculpted wood, which faced the interior garden courtyard. They were made by Telegu-speaking craftsmen at the JJ School of Art, and were meant to provide protection for the corridor from the weather. In addition, at the centre of the interior court, Stevens designed a fountain of great grace and charm.

An extension has been built to the original BMC, probably constructed in the 1950s or early 1960s. Stevens had planned for an extension, but he had suggested a Bridge of Sighs construction to link the two structures. What was built is not in the style nor does it have the flair that Stevens intended, and a plain ramp was inserted to join the two buildings instead. However, the offices still admirably serve their originally intended function and remain a symbol of civic pride for Bombay.

IN QUEST OF THE 'CORRECT' STYLE

MULJI JETHA FOUNTAIN

While the BMC building was still under construction, Stevens was called upon to work on a fountain dedicated to Ruttonsee Mulji's son, who was only fifteen years old when he died. Commonly referred to as the Mulji Jetha fountain, it is located at the intersection of Mint Road and P D'Mello (old Frere) Road. The commission was split between the sculptor Griffiths, principal of the JJ School of Art, and Stevens, who determined the overall scheme and provided the mechanical expertise.

At the apex of the fountain is a sculpture of the boy. Below him, an eight-columned octagonal pavilion with a round dome rises above a shallow basin at the second level. The bottom segment of the fountain comprises another set of eight columns above a larger pool. Around this pool, which served as a drinking trough for animals, Stevens placed four miniature domed pavilions, equidistant from one another. Two of the pavilions provide drinking-water fountains for the public. Numerous jets of water emanate from sculpted elephants' trunks and lions' heads or they just flow from open sprays as at the top.

The fountain was built with stone of various types: blue basalt for the large pool, white Porbandar with red granite columns for the two middle basins and the decorative details, blue granite for the uppermost level, and the lantern dome was composed of white stone.

The fountain was designed in the Indo-Saracenic style, and in 1892 this would have been Stevens's first attempt at working exclusively in this mode. The patron, a prominent Hindu citizen, may have requested the style. Aware of its growing importance, Stevens would have made a thorough study of Indo-Saracenic architecture, and the fountain commission would have influenced the design of his next major assignment, the BB&CI Railway Offices.

Mulji Jetha fountain in Indo-Saracenic style.

BOMBAY, BARODA & CENTRAL INDIAN RAILWAY OFFICES

Stevens faced no competition for the Bombay, Baroda and Central Indian (BB&CI) Railway's administrative office commission in 1893. His sterling work on VT for the rival GIP Railway had already made him the most sought-after architect in Bombay. The new site was across the street from the Churchgate Station, but the BB&CI (now Western) Railway had growing demands for office space as well as a desire for an imposing structure. Rao Sahib Siteram Khanderao and Charles F Stevens, the architect's eldest son who joined his father's firm in 1892, assisted on the project, and it was completed in 1899.

Built with basalt stone laid in courses, white Porbandar stone was employed for the domes, mouldings, capitals, columns, cornices and carved enrichments. The building's sculptural scheme was less elaborate than that of VT or the BMC building, but the ornamental woodwork, wrought iron details and furniture design were of a very high standard.

Centrally placed above three storeys of offices was a domed tower. The slightly irregular floor plan provided two *portes-cochère* and several pedestrian entrances, particularly on the western elevation, facing Churchgate Station. At the centre of each elevation was a gable terminated by a sculptural group commissioned from E Roscoe Mullins. The central

Line drawing of BB&CI Railway offices; skyline view of turrets and domes (below). BB&CI offices and Churchgate Station with Marine Drive being created (following pages).

Engineering *atop western gable of BB&CI offices.*

southern gable depicts *Engineering*, signified by a figure holding a train in her right hand and supported on the left by a cogwheel. Sculptured portrait roundels of Colonels PT French and MK Kennedy, pioneers of the railway company, were located over the western entrance. Griffins bearing the company arms adorn several smaller gables. Stevens placed a weather vane atop the central dome.

The interior has the pre-requisite external corridors, main staircase and corner staircases in corner towers, but with certain variations. No staircase was provided in the impressive central hall. Instead, the walls of the large square hall rose 100 feet, before modifying into an octagon to later bear the springing for the circular dome. This spectacular domed hall preserved its functional requirements by placing the principal staircase behind it. This is Stevens's fourth variant on a central hall plan and it continued his exemplary and innovative tradition of making the entrance hall the most important physical and social site within the structure. In a further refinement he placed the lift in the stairwell shaft's winding well, to save interior floor space, which could then be put to more practical use. Stevens's adoption of this plan was a probable result of the study he made of town halls for the earlier BMC building, as such an approach was common practice on the continent. Another planning feature, which paralleled his earlier building, was the water storage tank in the tower of the dome, its connection to the hydraulics of the lift, and the use of the additional two storeys, which the dome provided, for a record room. Though relatively symmetrical on the exterior, many variations in plan were incorporated within the interior to accommodate individual railway department needs. Thus, a strongbox was provided within the western block, a smaller division of the central block's largest ground floor rooms was planned, a library supplied, and so on.

Externally, the bulbous central dome's elevated profile was buttressed on the side in two stages from the square tower below. Distortions of scale and the overall massing's complexity give the building an Indo-Saracenic feel, but it is blended with the Venetian Gothic style, exemplified best by each individual dome's features. Here, the final appearance tends more towards the Indian because the numerous onion domes are accentuated in stark white. So, the offices actually chart new ground in a transitional architecture, which despite traditional Frere Town features of sprung arch openings on the ground floor and arcades with round arches above, blend into a whole with a distinctly novel appearance. In this way the building embodies architecturally Stevens's growing uneasiness over the correct choice of style. It also demonstrates his formidable powers to amalgamate styles in a successful whole.

Floor plan of BB&CI offices; note central hall with staircase behind.

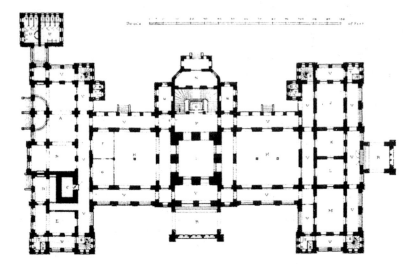

ARMY & NAVY COOPERATIVE SOCIETY STORE

Stevens adopted a variety of styles in his final years, unsure of either the neo-Gothic or the Indo-Saracenic style as a guaranteed lure for clients. In 1897, he went into partnership with David Ebenezer Gostling, a successful Bombay architect. Gostling brought a different clientele and expertise to Stevens's larger firm. Together they designed the four-storeyed Army & Navy Cooperative Society Store on Esplanade Road between Watson's Hotel and the David Sassoon Library. The offices of the Municipal Authority were formerly on this site.

Army & Navy Store's Italianate style main entrance front on Esplanade Road.

The store has a ground level round arch colonnade, which is open to and continues an arcade at street level, and the central four bays of its main elevation project slightly from the façade. A pediment at the centre of the composition bears both the store's coat of arms and a flagpole at its apex. The upper storeys are decoratively treated. A low balcony was applied to each floor, and different designs were employed at each floor level for the window architraves and pediments. Urns and two sculpted lions embellished the outer structure, with the store's name prominently spelt out. The building used a modified Italianate style with neo-Classical features. Constructed of red Vasai sandstone, the detailing was executed in grey marble. It is related in appearance to the Chartered Bank building.

CHARTERED BANK OF INDIA, AUSTRALIA & CHINA

FW Stevens died on 5 March 1900 while the building he designed for the Chartered Bank of India, Australia & China on Esplanade Road was still a work in progress. The bank commission may have stipulated its Italianate neo-Classical style.

Gostling & Stevens designed the offices in 1898, construction began in 1899, and the bank was completed at the end of 1902. The edifice provided for a banking hall, offices, a private apartment for the bank manager and his family, and servants' quarters at the rear. Supervised by

Decorative pediment with sculptural group of Great Britain, India, Australia and China above.

CF Stevens, the materials employed were Porbandar and light coloured basalt stone, and traditional ceramic tiles were used for the roofing.

The front or western elevation comprises a two-storey high tetrastyle central portico of the Corinthian order, raised on a rusticated ground floor one and a half storeys in height. The portico is contained within the elevation and it is enclosed on either side by solid masonry walls. Its pediment bears a flagpole at its apex and the coat of arms of the Chartered Bank, above which a sculptural group represents Great Britain, India, Australia and China. Behind the engaged columns of the portico two single-storey round arch arcades provide outdoor corridors and air circulation throughout the entire length of each floor. Alexander

Mackenzie & Co of the Byculla Saw Mills manufactured the interior woodwork, counters and furniture, and there was Minton tiling on the floors. Electricity and electric powered 'ventilating fans' were included in the original scheme as well.

Extensively remodelled in the 1990s, only some of the original features remain, primarily on the main façade and in those areas of the building still leased to tenants. With the death of FW Stevens, the firm of Gostling & Stevens was disbanded, but CF Stevens formed a new architectural partnership that evolved over time into the firm of Gregson, Batley & King. This firm still has its offices in the Chartered Bank building.

The floor plan of the building is a fairly complicated one, contained within a rectangular block, fifteen bays across and nine bays deep, with a courtyard or service area at the rear. There is no centralized staircase hall, in a break from Stevens's usual planning. Instead, two completely separate sets of stairs were provided, one located to the south of the main entrance. This private stair provided the bank with the opportunity to lease office space to commercial tenants, as their staff could gain access to a completely self-contained office block without disturbing the public entrance, vestibule and banking hall on the ground floor, all of which are used by the bank itself.

A second set of stairs, to the north, leads from the ground to the fourth floor, where the bank manager's private apartments were located. The accommodation comprised four bedrooms and four baths, in addition

Main western elevation in Italianate neo-Classical style; note engaged columns beneath pediment.

to various other reception rooms and servants' accommodation. Stevens's design also placed the banking hall centrally in the block, no doubt an important consideration in the scheme, and this hall's upper floors were serviced from the north stairs. Thus, with a complex ground plan Stevens enabled a clever pattern of circulation to be realised.

National Bank, now Standard Chartered Bank, 90 MG Road.

The placement and design of the banking hall further reaffirm the architect's formidable planning skills. By tucking the hall into a courtyard-like recess at the back of the building the architect could take full advantage of the extended ground floor height to give the interior space, air, and a sense of grandeur. Skylights illuminated the hall, relying upon the building's façade to reduce the impact of the afternoon sun. Thus, no direct light reached the hall when it was open for business. Similarly, a veranda above the hall allowed cooling breezes to enter the offices but blocked out the glare: a clever solution to a demanding set of needs.

In appearance, the bank would have rivalled one of its most likely business competitors, the National Bank (1867–74), also situated on Esplanade Road in a neo-Classical building designed by Scott & McClelland. However, the Chartered Bank building, built almost 30 years later, introduced a conflated scale and appearance appropriate to its own period of construction, which may in part be explained by the changed business climate of the two eras. The National Bank was constructed soon after the collapse of the 'cotton boom' when many individuals and companies were left bankrupt. Its solid structure would have radiated a sense of assured security. By contrast, the Chartered Bank building advertised the centralized location of a company, midway between London and East Asia, whose association with the furthest extent of the British empire greatly benefited the bank during a hugely prosperous era. It clearly exudes the confidence of an empire at the height of its powers.

BRITISH INDIA STEAM NAVIGATION BUILDING

The last building FW Stevens designed was the British India Steam Navigation (BISN) office on Nicol (R Kamani) Road. Construction, supervised entirely by CF Stevens, was begun in 1900 and completed in 1903. To what extent the architectural detail was left undetermined by his father is a matter for speculation, but it is likely that Charles had a substantial influence on the appearance of the building.

British India Steam Navigation building by Stevens on Nicol Road.

Now known as Kamani Chambers, the building is a square office block of four principal storeys, with four pronounced castellated corner towers that are each an extra storey in height. A pediment as high as the corner towers rises from the centre of the principal or eastern elevation, and below, at ground level, there is a *porte-cochère* and an entrance hall. A conventional floor plan clearly segregated work areas for the various departments, with offices for brokers, freight officials, and agents on separate floors. A manager's residence was provided on the uppermost floor. Rough cut Kurla stone was used as the primary building material with Porbandar stone for the window surrounds. Atypical in Stevens's oeuvre, the building was probably commissioned in the Scottish Baronial style by his client. This style derives from the traditional fortified domestic castle architecture of Scotland, but Stevens's composition was not very successful.

With commissions pouring into his office, Stevens's standards may have faltered. All his other buildings were carefully planned and were usually both attractive and practical. The BISN building, although of a satisfactorily functional design, is in an oddly inappropriate style and scale for its site. The neighbouring dockyard area is in the neo-Classical style and low scale. It is possible that CF Stevens altered or ignored his father's plan after his death.

ROYAL BOMBAY YACHT CLUB RESIDENTIAL CHAMBERS

Designed by Adams, the construction of the Royal Bombay Yacht Club
Residential Chambers was supervised by FW Stevens between 1896 and
1898. His son assisted him. The elder Stevens went to England in October
of 1898, which provides a firm date for completion of the project. The
building was very comfortably appointed with hydraulic lifts, electric
lights and fire services, and the engineering details were in keeping with
the high standards Stevens had established elsewhere. The architectural
design combined 'domestic' English neo-Gothic with a Tudor half-
timbered idiom and aptly demonstrated the disintegration of stylistic

cohesion that characterized turn-
of-the-century architecture in
Bombay. However, the Tudor half-
timbered style was also one in
which Adams had specialized, and it
harmonizes well with neo-Gothic
forms. In Britain of the period, this
mix was also quite traditional.

*Half-timbering and barge-board details of
RBYC Residential Chambers* (right). *The
building's eastern elevation* (below).

STEVENS DIED IN 1900, and he is buried at Sewri cemetery. The last few buildings described here indicate, within his own practice, the changed architectural climate of Bombay. One of Bombay's greatest and most significant architects, he understood the malaise and stylistic confusion consonant with his times. With his passing, the neo-Gothic era symbolically ended. There were undoubtedly a few more buildings erected in the neo-Gothic style after 1900, but the dean of its formal language had vanished from the scene. With Stevens's passing went the passion for Gothic, as would have suited its most able defender and gifted practitioner. His son CF Stevens went on to build Marshall & Sons at the corner of Ballard Road (Shoorji Vallabhdas Marg), the Civic Improvement Trust building (1902–04, now the Municipal ENT Hospital) at the intersection of Mayo Road (Bhaurao Patil Marg) and Esplanade Road, and the Orient Club (1910) on Chowpatty Seaface, among other projects.

CF Stevens's Marshall & Sons at Ballard Estate; note its Edwardian Baroque features.

CONCLUSION

AFTER FRERE INTRODUCED his development plan for Bombay, the PWD and various private architectural firms worked symbiotically to create a largely neo-Gothic urban fabric of similar and compatible appearance. Structures in newer or different styles, erected in Britain or elsewhere in India, had little impact on the appearance of Bombay's buildings. As a colonial dependency, Bombay was slow to change. The Indian community, which often funded construction costs, also underpinned its architectural preferences. Oriental forms were not perceived as the ideal answer to their Westernized tastes and aspirations. Other factors reinforced this pattern. TR Smith had advocated that the conqueror impose his own architectural style in India, citing this historic pattern in prior empires. The various Gothic styles employed in Bombay do relate both in appearance and in practice with contemporary structures in Britain. Magazines, photographs and the ease and frequency of travel between Bombay and Britain all contributed to the thorough and accurate dissemination of the latest design theories within India. The importation

Frere's portrait roundel on VT main office entrance elevation (left). *Deen Dayal's 1890s view of BMC at left and VT at right looking down Hornby Road* (below): *Stevens's ideal cityscape realised.*

Willcock's Anjuman-i-Islam School, a breakthrough Indo-Saracenic style building for Bombay.

of plans, architects, materials and capital to the city made the spread of such ideas possible on a scale never before attempted by a foreign 'conquering' people. In addition, the prevailing economic affluence and social confidence within the empire encouraged and maintained a self–

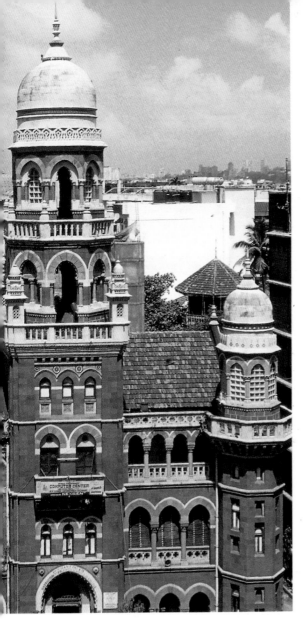

assurance that the British approach was essentially correct. However, even as the buildings began to be put to use, the collaboration necessary to construct them conspired to change their outward appearance.

Frere advocated the creation of an Anglo-Indian architecture when he proposed his master plan for Bombay, but he never intended to foster a polyglot form of architecture. He, too, wanted to fashion architecture along European lines, but with Indian craftsmen. However, the buildings of Bombay are, in many ways, unmistakably different from structures erected for similar uses in Britain. Some of these dissimilarities are naturally related to the climate and the construction materials employed, as even Smith had heartily argued that Gothic architecture had to be adapted to the climate and sunlight of the Indian subcontinent. Yet, as Smith and his fellow Victorians strove to achieve practical and rational solutions to the social and architectural problems of British India, an 'Architectural Art', styled especially for India, developed. It exults in a creative component,

visible in the buildings of Bombay, and unique to the city. Bombay's architecture is not self-generated, but the architects and artists that worked on its buildings did create a series of solutions to particularly Indian decorative and utilitarian needs.

The Victorians first employed science, engineering and imported products to solve their perceived architectural problems in India. But over time, creative architects who chose to work and live in the city became the dominant component that determined Bombay's appearance. Architects such as Emerson, Stevens, Adams and Murzban adapted the accepted theories of architecture to the particular needs of India. Emerson managed to convey some of Burges's stylistic features within a limited budget and a more restricted variety of materials. Even though he based his designs on European and British structures, Stevens was able to achieve a distinctive style of his own. The structures Adams designed were never identical to buildings in his favoured English Gothic style in Britain, and Murzban, his assistant and later competitor, was equally idiosyncratic in his

Edwardian Baroque style entrance door to George Wittet's JJ School of Art, architecture building (facing page). *Edwin Lutyens's Viceroy's House (Rashtrapati Bhavan), interior detail in the Edwardian Baroque style* (below); *note the theatrical spatial effects and clever massing.*

approach to Gothic form. Solutions to architectural problems in Bombay were creative but often also similar. The city's architectural circles were small and closely knit, opportunities for commissions were limited in contrast to fellow professionals in Britain, and there resulted a certain a homogeneity in approach.

Bombay Gothic's heyday ended for many reasons. As political events in India became associated with stylistic preferences in architecture and nationalism began to coalesce into a recognizable movement, the architectural profession responded accordingly. Thus, the study of earlier Indian architectural forms eventually led to a new respect for these historic models, and the large-scale projects of Bombay around the turn of the century and after reflect these new influences. Stevens's passing signified the end of neo-Gothic's primacy, though a few more structures

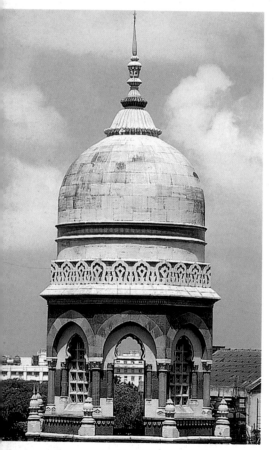

in the style were built. As older architects began to leave India or die, controversy plagued the architectural profession in Bombay and elsewhere. The younger architects who replaced them were actively looking for fresh solutions to stylistic and formal questions in architecture. In addition, stylistic preferences in architecture, related to political trends, were encapsulated by the national debate over Rashtrapati Bhavan's architectural form in the newspapers of the day. However, in Bombay, the Indo-Saracenic, Edwardian Baroque and Renaissance Revival styles prevailed as the civic architecture for about the next two decades. George Wittet was the leading practitioner of these latter styles in the city.

Willcock's Anjuman-i-Islam School, detail of Indo-Saracenic style cupola (1890-92).

APPENDIX

CENTRAL EVENTS

BOMBAY'S ARCHITECTURAL DEVELOPMENT

ARCHITECTURAL STYLES

ARCHITECTS & ARTISTS

CENTRAL EVENTS

FIRST GOTHIC REVIVAL BUILDINGS
Two men had a great impact on the appearance of Mumbai today: Henry Conybeare, an engineer and architect, and Bartle Frere, Governor of Bombay. Their collaboration on the Afghan Memorial Church (1847-58), resulted in a prototype Gothic Revival building for Bombay. The church has walls of stone in several colours, pointed arch stained glass windows, sloping tile roofs and fine wrought iron details within. Frere focused upon the architectural style to be used, Conybeare on how to achieve it.

MASTER PLAN
Frere went on to advocate the creation of an Anglo-Indian architecture. To establish this style at Mumbai he tore down the fort walls in 1862,

Sir Bartle Frere (1815-84).

liberating the city limits and allowing for extraordinary growth. By one act, he enabled the city centre to expand greatly. Frere then proposed a master plan for Bombay. The plan called for new public buildings, and all would be neo-Gothic in style. The buildings were in a European style, but they were built with Indian craftsmen trained to design in the novel style. The Sir Jamsetjee Jeejeebhoy School of Art, founded in 1854, produced craftsmen for this enterprise, and British architects and professors brought to Bombay realised Frere's dream of an Anglo-Indian architectural style.

GOTHIC TAKES SHAPE
In the 1870s and 1880s the High Gothic dream in Bombay took shape around the *maidans* of the city. Designed upon guidelines drawn up by a visiting British architect, Thomas Roger Smith, or based upon the work of leading British architects, such as George Gilbert Scott, the greater city of Bombay was largely made in the neo-Gothic style.

GOTHIC REVIVAL'S ZENITH
The finest of Bombay's architects in this style was FW Stevens. Known principally for his Victoria Terminus, he also designed the Bombay Muncipal Corporation building, the Bombay Baroda and Central India Railway offices and many other well-known structures in Bombay.

ECLECTICISM TAKES ROOT
As the end of the century approached, an uncertainty arose as to which architectural style was suitable for Bombay. Stevens died in 1900 as well, and the turn of the century shows both the style and his own practice decline in influence. Several important buildings that were constructed at this time bore evidence of an eclecticism that was popular in Edwardian Britain or was self-generated in India, and a new Classicism arrived in India, not only at New Delhi but throughout the subcontinent.

BOMBAY'S ARCHITECTURAL DEVELOPMENT

Bombay was a city thought unworthy of investment and effort, but it was transformed in role, function and appearance by Sir Bartle Frere and his administrative vision.

The proposals of the Bombay Government met with the full approval of the Secretary of State, who considered that the appropriation of the new ground to be acquired by the removal of the fortifications, or by reclamation, was a subject demanding special notice, and it was suggested that a comprehensive scheme should be drawn up in the first instance, and that no building lots should be sold, or otherwise disposed of, until not only the general arrangement, but also the style and character of the buildings to be erected, shall have been carefully considered, and a comprehensive plan matured in accordance therewith, and that, in framing such a plan, regard should be had not merely to the accommodation and convenience of the public, but also, in some degree, to architectural effect; and it was added that an opportunity, not likely to recur, will thus be afforded of building almost a new City in the Island of Bombay, and it may become a permanent subject of national reproach, if due advantage be not taken of it.

— *Government correspondence. Maharashtra State Archives, 1890-97*

When the English nation suddenly found itself the possessor of the great empire and of its great works of architecture, architecture in England was at such a low ebb that we could not realise what was essential to the progress of art in India. It was difficult to describe the general character of our early Anglo-Indian architecture; the only characteristic was extreme broadness – an utter absence of anything like distinctive features. This was only to be accounted for by the fact that we sent forth our representatives to receive and acquire the Indian Empire at about the same time as we were building Red Lion Square and the acres of featureless streets, roads, and squares, and the nightmare churches so unlike anything which is dreamt of as a church, whether in a town or a country village. Our ancestors in consequence left no good architecture behind them in India.

— *Sir Bartle Frere, in* The Building News. *Volume 18, 1870*

T R Smith described a prototype building for Bombay, in a speech before the RIBA on 27 April 1868, listing 'requirements' and 'design guidelines'.

It is almost self-evident that rooms should be large and airy, windows and doors so open as to admit every breeze that blows, yet so shaded as to keep out as much of the light as possible; and that walls should be far thicker than here, is necessary, and sheltered by some outer screen. Outside all the external walls, or at any rate, on all sides open to the sun's rays, a screen called a verandah is essential; and it becomes, in fact, the leading feature of buildings for the tropics. This may be best described as something like an external cloister, ordinarily about 10 ft wide, the roof usually running over it in a continuous line, and overhanging it. The verandah is, of course, often constructed of lighter materials than the main wall, but, where practicable, it is better to be of masonry. It is of course, desirable to have it as many stories in height as the building and covering most or all of the wall, but it admits of many variations, corbelling, projections, breaks, etc.

...In the day time the floor of the verandah, as indeed that of the rooms, is often sprinkled with water for coolness. These roomy appendages are not all lost space, advantage is taken of them when in shade, or catching the passing breeze, and then they serve as workrooms for native work people, or for lounging, smoking, walking, and even dining and sleeping in; Indian life being much al fresco, and privacy little studied, compared with comfort. The verandah...affords the chief, and a remarkably fine opportunity, for external architectural treatment in any building for the tropics. In some of the more artistic native houses, it is beautifully treated in carved wood. As an example of the treatment of it in masonry, I may refer to the Mahommedan buildings at Ahmedabad, shown in Mr. Hope's photographs, or to the fine design of Mr. Burges, for the Bombay School of Art. ...Allied to the verandah are corbelled balconies, and open oriels thrown out to catch the breeze and afford a cool evening nook; such features occur in the best Mohammedan work, and afford an excellent opportunity for picturesque treatment. ...The general plan of all buildings for the tropics ought to be, as will have been already understood, very simple, and at once compact and roomy. All servants reside apart, and few stores are kept in any house...The ordinary height of a storey is about 18ft. or 20ft.; and stairs being a serious fatigue in a hot climate, buildings of many stories are not common. An underground basement is not usual; it would become a harbour for vermin and filth, and would be flooded or damp in the monsoon (or wet) season. The ground floor is usually not less than 2 ft. or 3 ft. above the level of the surrounding earth and raised on a solid terrace. This height is, I believe, chiefly given as a protection against moisture, and hollow floors are avoided because vermin and snakes would be sure to get into them.

– The Builder, *1868*

It will be remembered probably, by some members of the Corporation that the style of architecture adopted for the Public Buildings erected on the Esplanade, commonly known as Frere Town, was decided upon by Sir Bartle Frere's Government, after careful deliberation and consultation with some of the most eminent architects in England and Bombay at that time. And I think the public of this generation should be much gratified at the result attained through the wise policy of the Bombay Government, in having followed out the lines then laid down...we think that the members of the Corporation will come to the conclusion we formed ourselves, that the new buildings, though not nearly so costly as the Terminus with which it is thoroughly in harmony, though quite different in mass and form, is every whit as effective as the Terminus itself, though necessarily simpler in detail.

– The Times of India, 4 March 1889

William Burges on French Gothic and 'muscularity' – a summary of the arguments for the style he popularized.

There was no doubt at all in Burges's mind that thirteenth-century Gothic represented the peak of medieval achievement. That century was 'the golden period of Christian art and poetry – the age which presented us with the Cathedral of Beauvais, the Abbey of Westminster, the Niebelungenlied and the Divine Comedy.'...For Burges, therefore, in the 1850s and even into the 1860s, Early French represented both a basis for the architecture of his own age and a springboard for the architecture of the future. 'Early French Art [is] more suited to the requirements of the present day than any other phase of Medieval architecture. We live under different conditions to our [medieval English] ancestors. They delighted in small pretty buildings, with delicate details, which would be out of place in our smoky atmosphere. In French art everything is upon a larger scale, and it is usually suited to our large warehouses and for high houses, such as are being sown broadcast in old London.' French Gothic was nobler, cheaper and characteristic of the modern age. 'The distinguishing characteristics of the Englishmen of the nineteenth century', Burges concludes, 'are our immense railway and engineering works, our line-of-battle ships, our good and strong machinery ...our free constitution, our unfettered press, and our trial by jury...[No] style of architecture can be more appropriate to such a people than that which...is characterised by boldness, breadth, strength, sternness, and virility.'

– *JM Crook,* William Burges and the High Victorian Dream, *1981*

ARCHITECTURAL STYLES OF THE 19TH CENTURY

ECLECTICISM

The 19th century formalized the view that it was justified to mine past architectural styles and use them, where appropriate, for any given building. This 'discovery' of a repository of styles established a great range of decorative options for architects of the period. In India, this led to the absorption of Hindu (Indo) and Mughal (Saracenic) architectural elements into neo-Gothic and neo-Classical compositions. Sometimes the buildings were pure enough in their

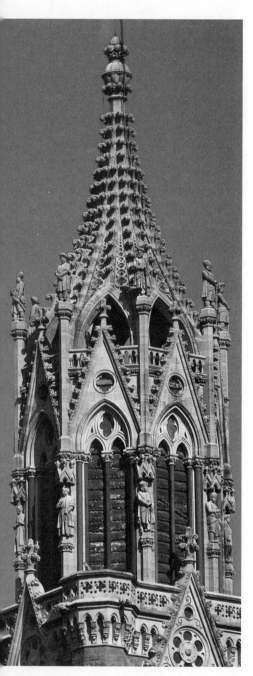

use of indigenous stylistic sources to be called 'Indo-Saracenic'; in other instances they were not, merely certain elements or certain areas of the building exhibited these unusually mixed stylistic characteristics.

GOTHIC

This style is associated with the medieval era in Europe, *circa* 1200-1530, when the traditions of the Classical civilizations of Rome and Greece were at their nadir and 'barbarians' dominated the politics of Europe. The pointed arch, the flying buttress, lancet windows, and a preference for stained glass are some of the hallmarks of the style.

English Gothic Scholars of the early 19th century divided the Gothic style, as practised in England, into three periods:

1. Early English, *c* 1190-1250. The first of what is known as the 'pointed' or Gothic style, it is more austere than what followed, and less costly to build.
2. Decorated, *c* 1250-1348. It was the preferred style of the Ecclesiologists.
3. Perpendicular, *c* 1350-1530.

Together with an earlier style that used round arches and massive construction, known as 'Norman' in England and 'Romanesque' in Europe, the Gothic style was a source of inspiration for 19th century architects. It came to be seen as the chosen style of the British when reconstructing the Houses of Parliament (1835-60). Many

Decorative lantern of Rajabai Tower.

British 19th century buildings used medieval forms in a style that came to be known as the Gothic Revival. This was just prior to Bombay's enormous building boom.

French Gothic in Bombay loosely combines French architectural forms, such as the *flèche*, with the Decorated style of English Gothic and its French equivalent. A more delicate, floriated and elaborate sculptural programme for windows, vaults, capitals and buttresses usually accompanies this style, in contrast to the plainer features of Early English edifices.

Muscular Gothic is a style that creates strong and unusual architecturally expressive elements in a composition. Elevations and details can appear over-scaled, clumsy and imbalanced, but this 'ugliness' is meant to achieve a masculine 'muscularity'. Although deliberately employing Gothic precedents, the buildings make no pretence of having actually been built in the medieval era. The heavy and massive forms of the Romanesque period are also inspirations for the style. As an extreme rejection of the Classical aesthetic, it adheres to the Pre-Raphaelite concept of 'truth to nature' by expressing a building's functions boldly on the exterior. Emerson and Molecey, influenced by William Burges, were frequent practitioners of this style.

Pre-Raphaelite is an English art movement founded with a 'brotherhood' (known as the PRB) in 1848. The artists, John Everett Millais, Holman Hunt, Ford Maddox Brown

Muscular turret of Emmanuel Church.

and others, wished to remove their art and aesthetic from that of the Royal Academy in London. They sought an earlier period in art, prior to Raphael, as their aesthetic model. Truth to nature, which meant a sometimes startling unvarnished or unimproved look to their subjects, bold pigments, *plein-air* painting and so on, was their credo. These 'honest' qualities were shocking to the Victorian public of the day: Christ really in a carpenter's shop, social veracity in depicting the various classes of Victorian Britain. Even the very idea of the brotherhood had medieval suggestions, which the public was intended to acknowledge. Ruskin sponsored the movement's artists in his writings, and their credo was very influential on later 19th century British artists.

Venetian Gothic John Ruskin, a very influential art critic and prolific writer of the Victorian era, popularized the architecture of Venice and the city's appearance through his drawings and writings. The style draws upon his critical insights and guidelines for its aesthetic choices. There is much use of arcaded façades wherein details are counterpointed in various coloured stones to create a textured and lively façade. Since the original sources were buildings designed for the bright sunlight of Venice, the principal features of this style were perfectly suited to reproduction in an Indian context.

ITALIANATE

This style refers to buildings, generally in the Classical tradition, which make use of motifs from the Roman period and from the early Italian Renaissance, as well as the traditional vernacular of Italy. It is a style common to domestic

Palazzo Contarini del Bovolo, late 15th century, Venice (left). GG Scott's University Library, staircase and arcade (1868-80), Bombay, in comparable style (right).

buildings of the 19th century, where the structures are most frequently of brick faced with stucco to imitate stone. Different varieties are sometimes named after the localities in Britain where they were first or most frequently used. The 'South Kensington Style' refers to the use of decoration derived from Italian Renaissance sources and frequently features are modelled in terracotta. This style was developed by the designers of the various museums in South Kensington, London, and widely copied in Britain. Rarely found in India, however its favoured material, terracotta, is not uncommon; and elements of the style can be identified in buildings such as those at the Bhau Daji Lad Museum and Zoological Gardens complex, or in the Army & Navy Store at Kala Ghoda and the Chartered Bank building on 23-25 MG Road.

ARCHITECTURAL STYLES OF THE EARLY 20TH CENTURY

RENAISSANCE REVIVAL

This was a style employed by George Wittet (1878-1926). It uses the architectural forms of the Italian Renaissance and avoids the use of stucco. The Institute of Science, the National Gallery of Modern Art, and the majority of the buildings on the Ballard Estate precinct are excellent examples in Mumbai.

EDWARDIAN BAROQUE

This style is characterized by an opulent, exaggerated use of forms and materials. Derived from 17th and 18th century European architecture of the late Renaissance and Mannerism, Wren, Hawksmoor, and Vanbrugh are its most famous practitioners in Britain. The style was based on theatrical effects and employs convex and concave flowing curves, optical illusions, exaggerated volumes, *et al*. The most famous examples in India are the Victoria Memorial Hall, Kolkata, and the buildings associated with New Delhi.

In Mumbai, Wittet's architecture school building at the JJ School of Art, CF Stevens's Marshall & Sons at Ballard Estate, and the Orient Club, Chowpatty Seaface, are other examples.

Edwardian Baroque features on the Orient Club by CF Stevens.

Looking across the Oval Maidan at Scott's Venetian Gothic University Buildings and the exaggerated massing of Fuller's High Court.

ARCHITECTS & ARTISTS

ADAMS, JOHN (1845-1920)

His output was quite extensive, and varied in style from half-timbered and Gothic Revival, to a polite Italianate, though the former predominated. In his 30-year career he built over 25 buildings in Bombay. The range of his work varied from providing hospital and educational buildings to undertaking religious commissions. When Adams joined the PWD in 1869, his first assignment was to design furniture for the Secretariat. Supervision of building work was an important component of his practice, when he was not himself designing the structures. He also executed several unbuilt proposals, for both Bombay and further afield in India. Examples of his buildings include Wilson College, the John Connon & Cathedral School buildings, the Royal Bombay Yacht Club and its Residential Chambers.

CONYBEARE, HENRY (1823-84)

Henry Conybeare developed an abiding interest in architecture from his father, WD Conybeare, the dean of Llandaff Cathedral in Wales. During Henry's adolescence, his father undertook a full restoration of the cathedral (between 1843-1882) with the assistance of the architect John Prichard (1817-86). The project site, prior to restoration, had an 18th century Classical church designed by John Wood (1704-1754) inserted within the ruined nave. The reconstruction of the Gothic fabric was most likely a topic of frequent if not daily conversation in the Conybeare household. Though the adult Henry Conybeare was by profession an engineer, he clearly possessed a deep interest in medieval architecture, reflected in the book he published on the subject, *The Ten Canons of Proportion and Composition in Gothic Architecture* (1868). The influence of his neo-Gothic St John's Church, Bombay, extended for several decades. Apart from designing the Vihar waterworks, the Tulsi reservoir system, and Love Grove Pumping Station, he also advised the Bombay government on matters regarding sanitation. His water and sewerage systems, at the forefront of health technology in his time, still service the city's needs, although Conybeare's remarkable contribution to Bombay's development seems to have been largely forgotten.

EMERSON, SIR WILLIAM (1843-1925)

After an education at King's College, London, Emerson trained with William Burges. On 7 July 1866 he arrived in Bombay with Burges's proposal for the JJ School of Art, and stayed on to work in the city, where apart from churches and the famous Crawford Market, he also planned the building for Treachers & Co. He won a silver medal at the Paris exhibition for his designs for the Muir Central College, Allahabad. His ultimate project was Calcutta's Victoria Memorial Hall. He was appointed president of RIBA in 1899, and received a knighthood in 1902.

FULLER, GENERAL JOHN AUGUSTUS (1828-1902)
Most of his career, which began with supervising St John's Church in Colaba, was spent in Bombay working within the PWD. He played a substantial role in several projects apart from the High Court, the David Sassoon Library, and the Gokuldas Tejpal Hospital.

GOSTLING & STEVENS (architectural firm)
The partnership of Gostling & Stevens was short lived. Soon after the Army & Navy Store and Chartered Bank buildings were designed and erected, Gostling formed another firm called Gostling & Chambers in 1902, and by 1905 this was called Gostling, Fritchley & Chambers. In 1907, the architectural firm Stevens & Co listed its members as CF Stevens, BG Triggs, and TS Gregson. This firm evolved into the present-day Gregson, Batley & King. CF Stevens continued his father's practice after his death, and built Marshall & Sons (corner of Ballard Road), the Civic Improvement Trust building (1902-04) at the intersection of Mayo and Esplanade Roads, and the Orient Club (1910) on Chowpatty Seaface. Gregson, Batley & King continues its practice in offices located in the Chartered Bank building.

JONES, OWEN (1809-74)
Born in London, Owen Jones trained with the architect Lewis Vuillamy and

Interior view of Iron Kiosk designed by Owen Jones.

at the Royal Academy. After travelling to Europe and the Near East in the years 1830-33, he returned to England for a career as colour printer and architect. In 1850 he was appointed joint architect of the Great Exhibition (Crystal Palace). Most of his buildings have now been demolished, but two of his villas at Kensington Palace Gardens, London, remain. An expert in polychromatic effects, he consulted on the Henry Cole staircase and related work at the Victoria & Albert (V&A) Museum, London. He published books on architecture, his 1856 *Grammar of Ornament* being one of the most important colour lithograph books of the 19th century.

KIPLING, JOHN LOCKWOOD (1837-1911)
Kipling studied at a school in Stoke, Staffordshire, administered by the V&A. Although his interest was in art, inculcated by a visit to the Crystal Palace Exhibition of 1851, Kipling came into contact with the architect GG Scott through the sculptor, J Birnie Philip, to whom he was apprenticed. Scott was working at the time on various Oxford college buildings. Kipling arrived in Bombay in 1865 as professor of architectural sculpture at the JJ School of Art. In 1875, he left for Lahore, where he was appointed principal of the Mayo School of Art. He returned to England in 1893.

MOLECEY, GEORGE TWIGGE
TR Smith was the first to suggest, with Governor Frere's encouragement, that GT Molecey travel out to Bombay to set up an architectural practice. He arrived in 1865 with Walter Paris, his

business partner, hoping to capitalize on the building programmes launched by the government. Molecey described himself then as a Gothic Revival architect. The firm of Paris & Molecey's first assignments were to draw up Trubshawe's Bombay projects. However, the partnership dissolved on 1 May 1867. By then Molecey had already accepted a teaching post at the JJ School of Art and, in 1870, the job of Architectural Executive Engineer with the government, a post that occupied him until his return to Britain in 1875.

During his tenure in India, Molecey adapted and made the final drawings for several other architects' designs. He was also able to construct several of his own designs, which included the present JB Petit School for Girls (1874-76) on Napier Road (M Dadhachi Road), partly overseen by Fuller after Molecey's departure for Britain; and the David Sassoon Building for the Elphinstone High School (1873-79) on Cruikshank Road. In collaboration with Paris, Molecey worked on the Telegraph Office in Bombay, the Callian Dispensary (1865) in Kalyan, and Christ Church (1866) in Kirkee. In Pune, he collaborated with Wilkins on St Paul's Church (1863-67), the Council Hall (1867), and the Ohel David Synagogue (1867-68).

MURZBAN, KHAN BAHADUR MUNCHERJEE COWASJEE (1839-1917)
Murzban was the only Indian architect of his era to achieve prominence for his architectural skill in Bombay. He began his career with the PWD, but by

the 1880s he had a flourishing private practice. Born in Bombay to an intellectual Parsi family, he travelled extensively in India and Europe. He built himself a large house called Gulestan on Murzban Road, and received the ennobling title of Khan Bahadur in 1877.

Murzban trained at the Poona Engineering College and began his career with the PWD in 1857. He came into daily contact with Frere on projects related to government work, and at Frere's request, he was appointed Trubshawe's assistant on the Ramparts Removal Committee in 1863. Murzban worked under TR Smith and was Fuller's special assistant. He was also responsible for photographing buildings erected by his department. As construction supervisor, Murzban oversaw the building of the General Post Office (1872), the Gokuldas Tejpal Native Hospital (1874), the Telegraph Office (1874), its extension wing (1888) and Signallers' Quarters (1878), the Sir Jamsetjee Jeejeebhoy School of Art (1878), the John Connon High School (1881), All Saint's Church, Malabar Hill (1882), Saint Mary the Virgin Church, Parel (1884), the Presidency Magistrate's Court (1886), the Dwarkadas Lallubhai Dispensary for Women and Children (1892), the Anjuman-i-Islam School of Bombay (1892), and the new Cathedral High School for Boys.

He also worked on the Cowasjee Jehangier Building for the Elphinstone College (1889), Byculla, in both a supervisory and an architectural capacity. He designed the The

Maharashtra State Archives building, and worked with Adams on the Miss Avabai Mehervanji Bhownagree Home for Nurses (1891, demolished 1985) and on the Lady Sakarbai Petit Hospital for Women and Children (1892).

ORDISH, ROWLAND MASON (1824-86) Having collaborated with Owen Jones on the Crystal Palace of 1851, Ordish was also involved in its construction and re-erection at Sydenham with Sir Charles Fox. He worked with GG Scott as an engineering consultant on the Holborn Viaduct (1863-69), and on the roof of St Pancras with Barlow (1866-68). His other assignments included the roof of the Albert Hall (1867-71), the Franz-Joseph Suspension Bridge (1869) over the Moldau in Prague, and immediately after the Bombay commission, the Albert Bridge, Chelsea (1872-73). He also worked on the Amsterdam station of the Dutch-Rhenish Railway in 1863, and devised the Winter Garden (1868) for an infirmary at Leeds by GG Scott.

PARIS, WALTER
Paris was an architect of no great distinction, but he was a prolific and skilled draughtsman. By the time his partnership with Molecey on the Ramparts Removal projects was dissolved, he had secured a job teaching architecture at the JJ School of Art, as the successor to Trubshawe. After several assignments in Bombay and elsewhere in the Western Presidency, he returned to London by 1 December 1872, where he set up

practice. There is no record of his work in India after this date. His career seems to have ended in the United States, as a watercolourist.

SCOTT, SIR GEORGE GILBERT (1811-78)
The son of a clergyman and himself evangelical, Scott first articled in 1827 with the architect James Edmeston, a like-minded religious friend of his father. During 1832-34 he worked for Henry Roberts, a pupil of Sir Robert Smirke (architect of the neo-Classical British Museum, 1823-47), a period in his career he disliked. With WB Moffatt, a builder's son, he designed and built over 50 workhouses, from the late 1830s to 1845. He also embarked on church designs, but it was not until 1841, with St Giles in Camberwell, London, that Scott felt he had achieved excellence in church design. The church was constructed in the Gothic style advocated by the Ecclesiologists. Scott went on to be appointed surveyor of Westminster Abbey in 1849. He restored numerous other cathedrals and colleges and hundreds of parish churches in Britain. He also designed many churches, colleges and public buildings.

Some of his most noteworthy and well-known commissions are The Albert Memorial, Hyde Park, London (1863), Glasgow University (1866-70), and the St Pancras Station (1868-74). Scott enjoyed an international reputation by the middle of his career, evidenced by his competition entries for the Cathedral of St John, Newfoundland (1840s), The Rathaus, Hamburg (1854) and The Parliament House, Berlin (1875) with JO Scott, or by his constructed Bombay University buildings (1868-1880) and a fountain in the churchyard of St Thomas's Cathedral paid for by CJ Readymoney (1866), among other projects.

He died leaving two famous architect sons to continue in his profession, John Oldrid Scott and George Gilbert Scott, Jr, whose own son Giles Gilbert Scott is also a famous architect. Giles Scott designed the Tate Modern/Bankside Power Station (1955) among other well-known works.

WILKINS, GENERAL HENRY ST CLAIR (1828-96)
Wilkins first practised in Pune, designing the Sassoon Hospital (1863-67), the Deccan College (1864-68), and with GT Molecey both the St Paul's Church (1863-67) and the Ohel David Synagogue (1867-68). They are all fine buildings, though the synagogue was judged at the time to be "the most striking building in Poona...The general effect of the building is rich and massive, and we venture to think that few Indian stations possess a non-official building, of modern date, fully equal to it." Wilkins also built Frere Hall (1863-65) in Karachi, as a memorial to Bartle Frere for services rendered in the province of Sind in the years 1850-59. Designed in an adapted Venetian Gothic style, the Hall provided a library and an auditorium for concerts and lectures. Wilkins also restored the ancient buildings at Bijapur, and built the Prag Mahal Palace at Bhuj (1865-75).

SELECT BIBLIOGRAPHY

DAVIES, PHILIP. *Splendours of the Raj, British Architecture in India, 1660 to 1947*. London: John Murray, 1985
— *The Penguin Guide to the Monuments of India. Vol. II: Islamic, Rajput, European*. London: 1989
DIXON, ROGER & S MUTHESIUS. *Victorian Architecture*. London: Thames & Hudson, 1978
NILSSON, STEN. *European Architecture in India, 1750-1850*. London: Faber & Faber Ltd, 1968
ROHATGI, PAULINE & P GODREJ & R MEHROTRA. *Bombay to Mumbai, Changing Perspectives*. Mumbai: Marg Publications, 1997

ON CHURCHES
CLARKE, BASIL FL. *Anglican Cathedrals Outside the British Isles*. London: Society for the Propagation of Christian Knowledge, 1958
HARRIS, JOHN AND JILL LEVER. *Illustrated Glossary of Architecture 850-1830*. London: Faber & Faber Ltd, 1966

ON ARCHITECTS
CROOK, JOSEPH MORDAUNT. *William Burges and the High Victorian Dream*. London: John Murray, 1981
GIROUARD, MARK. *The Victorian Country House*, Oxford: Clarendon Press, 1971
— *Alfred Waterhouse and The Natural History Museum*. London: Yale University Press, 1981
— *Cities and People*. New Haven & London: Yale University Press, 1985
IRVING, ROBERT GRANT. *Indian Summer: Lutyens, Baker and Imperial Delhi*. New Haven & London: Yale University Press, 1981

LONDON, CHRISTOPHER W. *Architecture in Victorian and Edwardian India*. Mumbai: Marg Publications, 1994
__ 'Architect of Bombay's Hallmark Style: Stevens and the Gothic Revival'. *Bombay to Mumbai, Changing Perspectives*, Pauline Rohatgi, P Godrej & R Mehrotra (eds). Mumbai: Marg Publications, 1997
— 'The Prag Mahal and Henry St Clair Wilkins' Architecture'. *The Arts of Kutch*. Mumbai: Marg Publications, 2000

ON PEOPLE
DOBBIN, CHRISTINE. *Urban Leadership in Western India. (Politics and Communities in Bombay City 1840 -1885)*. Bombay: Oxford University Press, 1972
GODREJ, PHEROZA J, & FIROZA PUNTHAKY MISTREE. *A Zoroastrian Tapestry*. Ahmadabad: Mapin Publishing Pvt Ltd, 2002
TINDALL, GILLIAN. *City of Gold*. London: Temple Smith, 1982

ON BOMBAY & HISTORY
DOSSAL, MARIAM. *Imperial Designs and Indian Realities; The Planning of Bombay City 1845-1875*. Bombay: Oxford University Press, 1991
EVENSON, NORMA. *The Indian Metropolis: A View Toward the West*. New Haven: Yale University Press, 1989
MURRAY, JOHN. *Handbook for India*. London: John Murray, 1978
SPEAR, PERCIVAL. *The Oxford History of Modern India 1740-1975*. Delhi: Oxford University Press, 1978

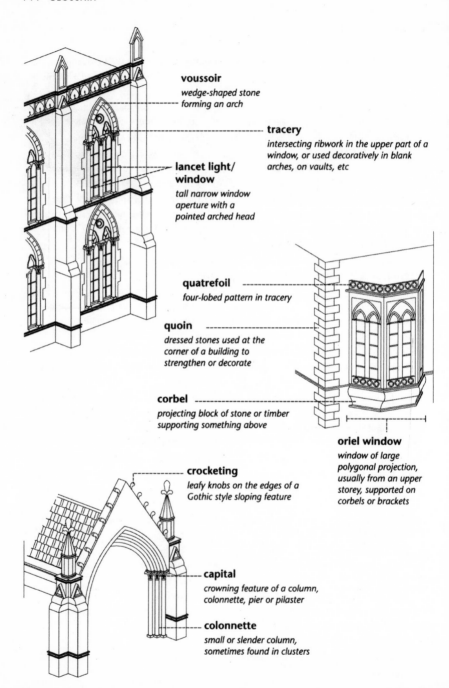

voussoir
wedge-shaped stone forming an arch

tracery
intersecting ribwork in the upper part of a window, or used decoratively in blank arches, on vaults, etc

lancet light/ window
tall narrow window aperture with a pointed arched head

quatrefoil
four-lobed pattern in tracery

quoin
dressed stones used at the corner of a building to strengthen or decorate

corbel
projecting block of stone or timber supporting something above

oriel window
window of large polygonal projection, usually from an upper storey, supported on corbels or brackets

crocketing
leafy knobs on the edges of a Gothic style sloping feature

capital
crowning feature of a column, colonnette, pier or pilaster

colonnette
small or slender column, sometimes found in clusters

STREET NAMES – OLD & NEW

Apollo Pier Road: *Chhatrapati Shivaji Marg*
Ballard Road: *Shoorji Vallabhdas Marg*
Carnac Road: *Lokmanya Tilak Road*
Church Gate Street: *Veer Nariman Road*
Colaba Causeway: *Shahid Bhagat Singh Road*
Cruickshank Road: *Mahapalika Marg*
Esplanade Road: *Mahatma Gandhi (MG) Road*

Frere Road: *P D'Mello Road/Shahid Bhagat Singh Road*
Grant Road: *Maulana Shaukatali Road*
Hornby Road: *Dr Dadabhai Naoroji (DN) Road*
Marine Drive: *Netaji Subhas Chandra Road*
Mayo Road: *Bhaurao Patil Marg*
Napier Road: *M Dadhachi Road*
Nicol Street: *R Kamani Road*

ILLUSTRATIONS   *A listing of archival material*

Inner Front Cover *Frere Town.* Drawing by Manisha Shah

6-7 High Court and Rajabai tower. Albumen Print. *c* 1880

10-11 The Mint (1829). Postcard. Alpiawalla Museum, Mumbai

13 **(top right)** Benedictine Kitchen, Marmoutier, France. Reproduced in Joseph Mordaunt Crook, *William Burges and the High Victorian Dream.* 1981; **(bottom)** Sir JJ Hospital (1846). Watercolour. Bhau Daji Lad Museum, Mumbai

15 Same as page 13 (bottom)

17 Afghan Church. *Memorial Church Colaba, H Conybeare (1846).* Engraving. Reproduced in Henry Conybeare, *The Ten Canons of Proportion and Composition in Gothic Architecture, Established by an Analysis of the Best Medieval Examples, and Practically Applied to the Design of Modern Churches.*1868

20 Sir Jamsetjee Jejeebhoy Bt. (1783-1859). Oil on canvas. 117 x 97 cms. Jamsetjee Jejeebhoy Parsee Benevolent Institution, Mumbai

21 Proposal for the JJ School of Art. Drawing by William Burges. Reproduced in Joseph Mordaunt Crook, *William Burges and the High Victorian Dream.* 1981

22-23 Proposal for the JJ School of Art. Drawing by William Burges. 1866. British Architectural Library, RIBA, London

24 **(top)** Same as page 13 (top right)

26-27 *Plan of the Fort and Esplanade of Bombay. 1827.* Maritime History Society, Mumbai

28 HBE Frere (1815-84). Portrait

29 North Side elevation of University clock tower and library. Drawing by Vikas Dilawari

31 *Watson's Building, Bombay. RM Ordish, Engineer & Architect.* Lithograph by J Emslie & Sons, London. Reproduced in *The Architect*, Vol 1. 1869

32 Proposal for Iron Kiosk. Drawing by Owen Jones. Reproduced in *The Builder*, Vol 24. 1866

33 *Watson's Building, Bombay. Details of Ironwork. RM Ordish, Engineer & Architect.* Lithograph by J Emslie & Sons, London. Reproduced in *The Architect*, Vol 1. 1869

34 Watson's Hotel. Postcard. *c* 1920

36-37 Skyline with the High Court, Oriental Buildings and BMC offices. Photograph by Deen Dayal. *c* 1900

38-39 The Secretariat. Photograph. *c* 1880

40 View of the Convocation hall, library and clock tower. Photograph by Deen Dayal. *c* 1880

42 **(centre)** Floor plan of the University library. Drawing by Vikas Dilawari

44 **(top left)** *Shri Premchand Roychund* and **(top right)** *Smt Rajabhai Roychund.* Oil on canvas by VB Pathare. 1986. University of Mumbai collection

45 West elevation of University library and clock tower. Drawing by Vikas Dilawari

48 **(bottom)** *The Sir Cowasjee Jehanghier Hall of the University of Bombay. Sir GG Scott, RA, Architect.* Engraving. Reproduced in *The Builder*, Vol 34. 1876

52 **(top)** General John Augustus Fuller. Photograph. *c* 1900

55 PWD building. Engraving. Reproduced in *The Builder*, Vol 32. 1874

56 General Post Office. Photographer unknown. *c* 1872

61 *Elphinstone College, Bombay – Mr. James Trubshawe, Architect.* Engraving by Maguire(?) after a drawing by LM Williams. Reproduced in *The Builder*, Vol 24. 1866

62 Crawford Market. Postcard. *c* 1920

64 **(bottom)** *Market Fountain, Bombay. W Emerson – Architect.* Lithograph by James Akerman after a drawing by Maurice B Adams. Reproduced in *The Building News*, Vol 27. 1874

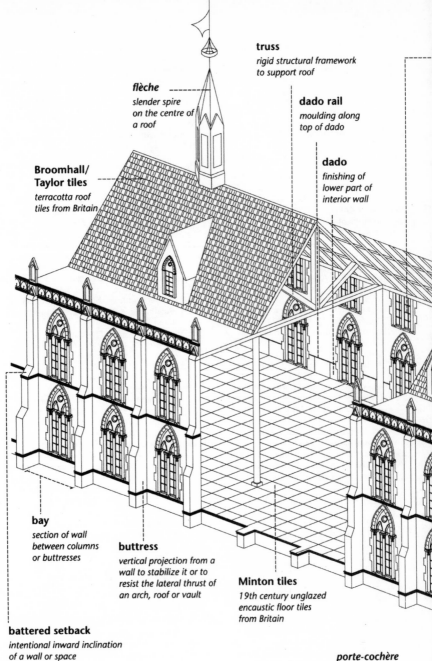

truss
rigid structural framework to support roof

flèche
slender spire on the centre of a roof

dado rail
moulding along top of dado

dado
finishing of lower part of interior wall

Broomhall/ Taylor tiles
terracotta roof tiles from Britain

bay
section of wall between columns or buttresses

buttress
vertical projection from a wall to stabilize it or to resist the lateral thrust of an arch, roof or vault

Minton tiles
19th century unglazed encaustic floor tiles from Britain

battered setback
intentional inward inclination of a wall or space

porte-cochère
porch large enough for a carriage to pass through

clerestory
uppermost storey of the nave walls of a church, pierced by windows

gable
upper part of wall, closing the end of a pitched roof

finial
ornament at apex of a pinnacle

dormer window
projecting upright window set vertically in a sloping roof

rose window
circular window with foils of patterned tracery arranged like spokes of a wheel

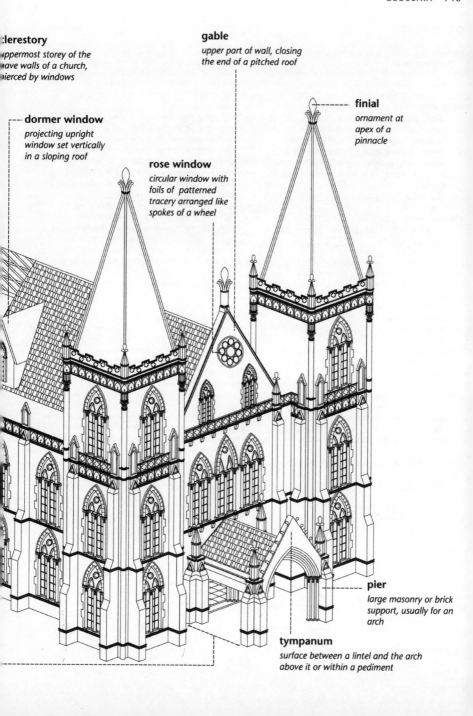

pier
large masonry or brick support, usually for an arch

tympanum
surface between a lintel and the arch above it or within a pediment

GLOSSARY

architrave: moulded frame for doorway, window or arch

barge-boards: boards, often carved or fretted, fixed beneath the eaves of a gable to cover and protect rafters

bar tracery: strips of stone across an opening

bressumer: prominent horizontal beam, usually set forward from the lower part of a building, supporting the wall above

Broomhall tiles: red terracotta roof tiles from Britain, with an interlocking pattern on the lower surface to reduce breakage and other damage

chhajja: projecting eave providing shade to the wall below

chunam: Indian lime plaster or mortar, produced from burnt powdered shells or other substances

cupola: rounded dome forming a roof or ceiling, or sometimes adorning a roof

dovetailed ribs: a projecting band on a ceiling or vault, separating the cells of a groined vault, joined to the next by a projecting piece fitting into a socket

elevation: any side or face of a building

engaged column: one that is partly merged into a wall or pier

flying buttress: transmits the outward thrust to a heavy abutment by means of a vault, arch or half-arch

groin vaulting: four curving triangular surfaces or sections produced by the junction of two tunnel vaults at right angles; the curved lines at the intersections are called *groins*

half-timbering: non-structural decorative timber-work contrasted with another material, eg in gables

leaded lights: coloured and/or plain glass (not stained) windows with panes secured in a lattice made of lead

Minton tiles: extensively used 19th century unglazed encaustic floor tiles manufactured in Britain, revived from medieval examples of solid colours for each pattern

mullion: vertical member between lights of a window opening

multifoil: more than six lobes formed by cusping of a circular or other shape in tracery (*foil*: leaf); similarly, *trefoil* (three), *quatrefoil* (four), and *cinquefoil* (five) lobes

overdoors: painting or relief above a door

pediment: in Classical architecture, a low-pitched triangular gable form over a portico or façade; also used over doors, windows, etc

poppoi: Indian term for Gothic form based on 15th-16th century poppy-head finials often richly decorated with figures, foliage, fruits and flowers; derived from the French *poupée* (a bunch of hemp or flax tied to a staff)

pylon: any isolated structure used decoratively or to mark a boundary

Ransome's Patent Stone: ground stone set with fine lime cement in a mould to take specific shapes, with the colour and durability of sandstone or limestone, but more economical than carved stone

reredos: painted and/or sculptured screen behind and above an altar

rib vaulting: any vault with an under-surface divided by moulding or ribs

rusticated: stone masonry with a textured roughened surface to express power and solidity

squinch: arch or series of arches thrown across an angle between two walls to support a superstructure of polygonal or round plan over a rectangular space, eg a dome

Taylor tiles: terracotta roof tiles made in 19th century Britain

transom: cross-bar or beam

Architectural definitions adapted from Nikolaus Pevsner, The Buildings of England, *Penguin Books; John Fleming, Hugh Honour, Nikolaus Pevsner,* The Penguin Dictionary of Architecture *(1991); James Stevens Curl,* Dictionary of Architecture, *Oxford University Press (1999).*

ABBREVIATIONS

BB&CI	Bombay, Baroda & Central India Railway	JJ	Jamsetjee Jeejeebhoy
		PWD	Public Works Department
BISN	British India Steam Navigation	RBYC	Royal Bombay Yacht Club
BMC	Bombay Municipal Corporation	RIBA	Royal Institute of British Architects
CJ	Cowasjee Jehangir		
GPO	General Post Office	VT	Victoria Terminus

CONVERSIONS

1 foot *0.3048 metre*   **1 inch** *2.542 centimetres*

72   Elphinstone High School. Photograph.
      Reproduced in James H Furneaux, *Glimpses
      of India*. 1895
76   Rear view of Chief Presidency Magistrate's
      Court (*c* 1900). Postcard. Alpiawalla
      Museum
78   Frederick W Stevens. Photograph. *c* 1900
79   Victoria Terminus, main and east
      elevations. Photograph. *c* 1900
80 & 85 The great Indian Peninsula Railway
      Terminus and Offices. Watercolour by
      Axel Herman Haig. 90 x 155cm. *c* 1878.
      The British Library, London
81-82 St Pancras Station, London. Photograph
      by Bedford Lemere. *c* 1890. English
      Heritage, National Monuments Record,
      London
83-84 VT Station. Photograph by Deen Dayal.
      c 1900
99   *Municipal Buildings Bombay. West elevation
      facing Cruikshank Road. Drawing by
      Frederick W Stevens. Reproduced in
      The Building News*, Vol 59. 1890
102   Interior Cross section of BMC entrance
      hall, staircase and double dome.
      Lithograph by James Akerman after
      a drawing by Frederick W Stevens.
      Reproduced in *The Building News*,
      Vol 59. 1890
104   Interior cross section of BMC hall. Drawing
      by Vikas Dilawari
106   Ruttonsee Mulji Memorial Fountain.
      Lithograph by James Akerman after

a drawing by FW Stevens. Reproduced
in *The Building News*, Vol. 64, 1893
107   *New Administrative offices. Bombay-Baroda
      & Central India Railway at Bombay,
      FW Stevens*. Photo-tint by James Akerman.
      Reproduced in *The Building News*,
      Vol. 70, 1896
108-109 BB&CI offices and Churchgate Station.
      Photograph by Deen Dayal. *c* 1900
111   Floor plan of BB&CI offices. Same as
      page 107
115   Bombay National Bank, front view.
      Postcard. Photograph by Phototype
      Company. *c* 1900-10. Alpiawalla Museum
116   British India Steam Navigation building.
      Postcard. *c* 1910. Alpiawalla Museum
117   (bottom) Eastern elevation of RBYC
      Residential Chambers. Photograph.
      c 1890
119   (top left) Detail from page 120
120-121 BMC and VT. Photograph by
      Deen Dayal. *c* 1900
136-137 High court, clock tower and
      Convocation hall across the Oval Maidan.
      Photograph. *c* 1880
139   Interior view of Iron Kiosk. Drawing.
      Reproduced in *The Builder*, Vol 24. 1866
144-146 Elevation drawings by Sunita Dalvi
150-151 *Fort and Esplanade, Bombay. Birds Eye
      View showing proposed arrangements.*
      Lithograph by James Trubshawe. May
      1864. The British Library, London

CREDITS

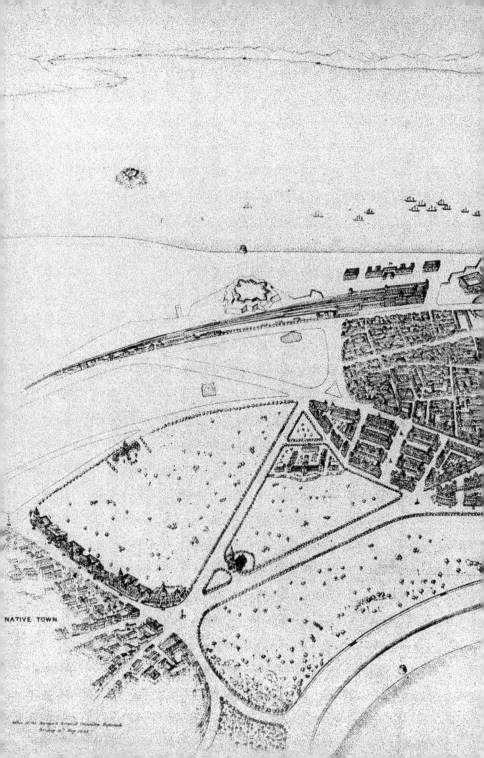

NATIVE TOWN

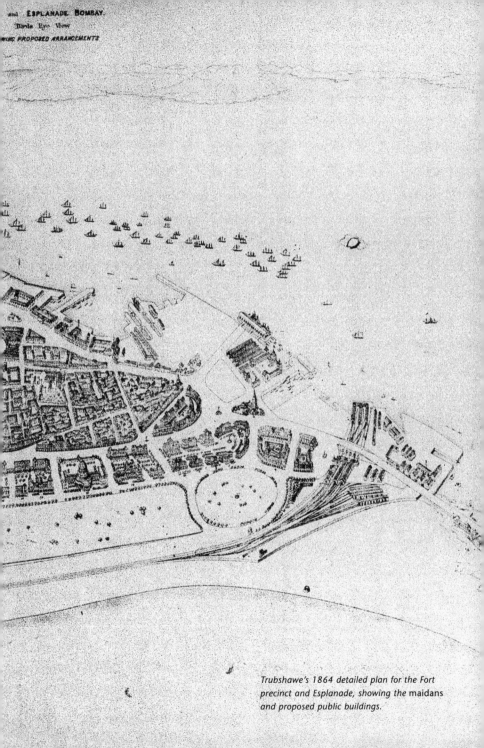

and ESPLANADE BOMBAY.
Birds Eye View
NING PROPOSED ARRANGEMENTS

Trubshawe's 1864 detailed plan for the Fort precinct and Esplanade, showing the maidans and proposed public buildings.

INDEX *Page numbers in bold refer to illustrations*

Adams, John, 125, 138
collaboration with Stevens, 78, 101, 117
furniture design, 38
Magistrate's Court, 75-76
RBYC Residential Chambers, 117
Afghan Memorial Church. *See* St John's Church
Aitken, Russell, 62, 64
Alexander Mackenzie & Co, 114
All Saint's Church, 141
Ambroli Mission Church, 71
American Civil War, 25
Andrew Handyside & Co, 31
Anglo-Indian architecture, 29-30, 37, 123
guidelines, 28, 128, 129-130
Anjuman-i-Islam School, **122**, 141
cupola, **126**
Apollo Pier Road, 100
'Architectural Art', 123
Architectural Association, 29
Architectural Society of Oxford, 16
Army & Navy Store, 112, 135, 139
Azad Maidan, 37, 72, 75
Back Bay, 32, 40
Ballard Estate, 135
Ballard Road, 118
Banias, 30
banqueting hall style, **42**
Bapoojee, Wassoodeo, 54
BB&CI offices, 106, 107-111, 128
Berkeley, James J, 93
Bhatia Shets, 30
Bhau Daji Lad Museum, 60, 135
Bhaurao Patil Marg. *See* Mayo Road
BISN, 116
Birmingham Council Chamber, 105
BMC building, **37**, 98, 99-106, 107, 110, **120**
battle of styles, 98, 99-101
Corporation Hall, **104**, 105
double dome, **102**, 104
Stevens's design, **99**, 101-105
Bombay
architectural development, 129
architectural stone, 18, 30
British ownership, 10
development, 15, 25-28
financial collapse (1865), 23, 25, 65, 115
fort, 25, **26-27**, 28, 36, 128
Bombay Baroda and Central India Railway Offices. *See* BB&CI
Bombay Muncipal Corporation building. *See* BMC

Bombay Special Fund, 30
Bombay Builder, The, 17
Boulton, Richard Lockwood, 96
Neptune plaque, **97**
British India Steam Navigation. *See* BISN
Broomhall tiles, 38, 57
Brown, Ford Maddox, 133
Builder, The, 100, 130
Building News, The, 25, 129
Burges, William, 11, 15, 29, 31, 130
draughtsman Haig, 79, 86
French Gothic style, 22, 131
JJ School proposal, 21-23, 24, 138
muscularity, 131
student Emerson, 63, 64, 65, 67, 68, 125, 133
Butterfield, William, 17, 18
Campbell, John, 58
cast iron
architecture, 31-34
lamp brackets, 64
Cathedral School, 72, 138
Catherine of Braganza, 10
Central Railway. *See* GIP Railway
Central Telegraph Office, 56. *See also* GPO
Charles II of England, 10
Chartered Bank building, 112, 113-115, 135, 139
chhajja, 57, 97
Chhatrapati Shivaji Marg. *See* Apollo Pier Road
Chhatrapati Shivaji Terminus. *See* VT
Chief Presidency Magistrate's Court, 75-76
flèche, 76
stonework, **74**
Chisholm, Robert Fellowes, 34, 98, 99-101
chunam, 15, 18
Church Gate Street, 54, 61
Churchgate Station, **108**
Civic Improvement Trust building, 118, 139
Clerk, Sir George Russell, 50
Colaba Causeway, 96
Convocation Hall, Bombay University, **40**, 45-51
interior, **51**
multifoil window, **25**
rose window, **50**
Conybeare, Henry, 16-19, 20, 128, 138

Conybeare, WD, 138
Corporation Hall, BMC, 105
cross-section, **104**
cotton boom, 25
collapse, 23, 65, 115
Council Chamber, BMC, 101
Crawford, Arthur Travers, 62, 66
armorial, **66**
Crawford, CEG, 70
Crawford Market, 62-66, 89, 138
cast iron brackets, 64
design, 62-63
fountain, **64**, 65-66
original plan, 62
stone materials, 64
style, 64-65
Crook, Joseph M, 22, 131
Cross Maidan, 37
Cruikshank Road, 72, 75, **99**, 103, 140
Crystal Palace. *See* Great Exhibition
David Sassoon Library & Reading Room, 58-59, 112, 139
de Forest, Lockwood, 98
Decorated style, 14, 132, 133
Dilawari, Vikas, 105
domestic English style, 117
domestic Gothic style, 96
double roof technique, 22, **32**
dovetailed ribs, 86
DN Road. *See* Hornby Road
Early English style, 14, 132, 133
bar tracery, 43, 48
High Court, 52
St John's Church, 18
Earp, Thomas, 87, 90, 92
East India Art Manufacturing Co, 90
Ecclesiological Society, 14, 16, 132, 142
eclecticism, 11, 128, 131
Edmeston, James, 141
Edwardian Baroque style, **118**, **124**, 126, 135
Elphinstone, Lord, 92
Elphinstone, Mountstuart, 60, 93
Elphinstone College, Byculla, 51, 60-61, 62, 141
Elphinstone High School, 72-73, 140
dome, **14**
Elphinstone Institution, 21
Emerson, Sir William, 125, 133, 138
Ambroli Mission Church, 71
armorial, **66**
Burges's influence, 64, 65

Emmanuel Mission Church, **68**, 69-71
fountain design, **64**, 65-66
French Gothic style, 64, 67, 68
JJ School drawings, 22, 23, 63
lamp brackets, 64
market design, 62-63
muscular Gothic style, **66**, **68**, 133
St Paul's Church, 67-68
Emmanuel Mission Church, **68**, 69-71
Engineering sculpture
VT, 91
BB&CI offices, 110
English Gothic style, 125, 132-133
Early English, 14, 18, 43, 48, 52, 132, 133
Decorated, 14, 132, 133
domestic, 117
Perpendicular, 132
Esplanade Hotel. *See* Watson's Hotel
Esplanade (Mahatma Gandhi) Road, 31, 34, 112, 113, 115, 118, 135
European General Hospital, 29, 78
Fitzgerald, Sir Seymour, 50
flèche, 14, 76, 133
floor tiles. *See* Minton tiling
Fort area, **26-27**, 30, 60, 61
fort walls, 25, 28, 36, 128
fountains
BMC, 105
Crawford Market, **64**, 65-66
Elphinstone College, **61**
Mulji Jetha, 106
Rusi Mehta Chowk, **66**
VT, 89
French, PT, 110
French Gothic style, 15, 22, 65, 67, 68, 133
High Court window, **14**
influence on Adams, 76; Burges, 22, 131; Emerson, 65, 67, 68
Frere, Sir Henry Bartle Edward, 58, 62, 98, 128, 130, 141, 142
Anglo-Indian architecture, 29, 123, 129
Bombay's motto, 16, 103
coat of arms, **25**, 38, 50
collaboration with Conybeare, 16-17, 18, 128
iron trade connection, 34
plan for Bombay, 16, 20, 25-30, 36-37, 38, 56, 60, 129, 130

portrait roundel, 93, 120
Frere Road, 96, 106
Frere Town, 58, 59, 101, 130
architectural materials, 57
definition, 36-37
sprung arch features, 111
Fuller, General John Augustus, 139, 141
David Sassoon Library, 58, 59
Elphinstone College, 60
High Court, 41, 52-54, **136**
JB Petit School for Girls, 140
JJ School of Art, 24
St John's, 17
Gaekwad Sayaji Rao II, 96
gargoyles, **46**, 48, **69**, 93, **95**
Geary, Grattan, 101
General Post Office. *See* GPO
Gibello, stone contractor, 90
GIP Railway, 15, 28, 79, 107
coat of arms, **93**, **94**
Glasgow Municipal Building, 105
Gokuldas Tejpal Hospital, 139, 141
Gomez, master sculptor, 90
Gol Gumbaz, Bijapur, 105
Gostling & Stevens, 139
Gostling, David Ebenezer, 112, 113, 114, 139
Gothic style, 14, 132-134
British practitioners, 29, 138, 142
development in Bombay, 30, 51, 123, 128
domestic, 96
features, 10-11, **19**, 51
Gothic Revival, 17, 133
banqueting hall style, **42**
Bombay architects, 29, 30, 78, 128, 138, 140
Bombay buildings, 20, 98, 128
theorists, 11
Government House, 101
GPO, 54, 56-57, 78, 97, 141
Grant Medical College, 15
Grant Road, 69
Great Exhibition (1851), 20, 22, 32, 33, 140, 141
Great Indian Peninsula Railway. *See* GIP Railway
Gregson, Batley & King, 114, 139
Griffiths, John, 90, 106
groin vaulting, 42, 48, **88**, 89
Growse, Frederick Salmon, 98
Haig, Axel Herman, 86
VT perspective, 79, **80**, **85**
half-timbered style, 117, 138
Hatwood, James, 33
Hawksmoor, Nicholas, 135
Heaton, Butler & Bayne Ltd, 41, 51

Hemnagar stone, 38
Hems, artist, 104
Higgins, MJ, 21, 70
High Court, **36-37**, 39, 40, 52-54, 55, 76, **136**, 139
window tracery, **14**
Hindu architecture, 29, 30, 99, 131
Holland, Colonel, 93, **94**
Hope, TC, 22
Hornby Road (Dadabhai Naoroji Road), 21, 103, **120**
Houses of Parliament
Berlin, 87
London, 132
Hunt, Holman, 133
Hunter, Alexander, 20
Hyde, General, 45
Indo-Saracenic style, 131, 132
Anjuman-i-Islam School, **122**, **126**
Army & Navy Store, 112
BB&CI office, **107**, 111
Chisholm's position, 98, 99, 100
Mulji Jetha fountain, 106
BMC building, 99, 100, 104
Institute of Science, 135
Iron Kiosk, 31-32, **139**
Italian Gothic, 15, 22, 93, 103. *See also* Venetian Gothic
Italianate style, 112, 113, 114, 134, 135, 138
J Macfarlane & Co, 96
Jain patrons, 30, 40
jalis, 22, 105
Janardhan, Mahderao, 87
JB Petit School for Girls, 140
Jeejeebhoy, Sir Jamsetjee, 20, 92
JJ School of Art, 20-24, 128, 141
architecture school building, **124**, **135**
Burges's proposal, 22-24, 63, 138
ironwork, 18, 96
principal, 90, 106
sculpture, 51, 75, 90
teachers, 20-21, 140
wood carving, 105
John Connon High School, 141, 138
John Taylor & Co, 44
Jones, Owen, 22, 23, 29, 31, 32, 139
Justice sculpture, **52**, 53
Kamani Chambers, 116
Kennedy, MK, 110
Khanderao, Siteram, 87, 107
Kipling, John Lockwood, 21, 51, 58, 60, 70, 140
armorial, **66**

Crawford Market sculpture, 62, 63, 65,
Sailors' Home sculpture, 96,
Indian designs, 98
Kurla stone, 18, 24, 30, 38, 41, 57, 59, 64, 65, 66, 70, 71, 73, 97, 116
Kutch stone, 30
lancet windows, 11
Convocation Hall, 50, 51
Emmanuel Church, 70
High Court, 53
Magistrate's Court, 75, 76
St John's, 17, **18**
University Library, **41**, 42
VT, 87
library. *See* David Sassoon Library; University Library
Love Grove Pumping Station, 138
Lutyens, Edward, Viceroy's House, **125**
M Dadhachi Road. *See* Napier Road
Magistrate's Court, **74**, 75-76, 141
Mahapalika Marg. *See* Cruikshank Road
Maharashtra State Archives, 129, 141
Mahendra Mansion, 34
Mannerism, 135
Mant, Sir Charles, 43
Marine Drive, **108-109**
Marochetti, Carlo, 20
Marshall & Sons, 118, 135, 139
Maw & Co, 89
Mayo Road, 118
Mechanics' Institute, 21, 58
Mercy sculpture, **52**, 53
MG Road, 115, 135. *See also* Esplanade Road
Millais, John Everett, 133
Mint, **10-11**, 15, 106
Minton tiling, 18, 34, 38, 41, 45, 57, 58, 59, 70, 73, 114
Moffatt, WB, 142
Molecey, George Twigge, 133, 140, 141, 142
JJ School of Art, 23-24
university, 41, 48, 50
High Court, 52
Elphinstone College, 60
Elphinstone High School, 72-73
Mughal architecture, 22, 29, 30, 99, 131
Mullins, E Roscoe, 107
Mumbai, 128, 135. *See also* Bombay
Municipal Act (1865), 62
Municipal Authority, 99, 112

Municipal ENT Hospital. *See* Civic Improvement Trust building
Murzban, Khan Bahadur Muncherjee Cowasjee, 24, 56, 58, 75, 125, 140
muscular Gothic style, 15, 131, 133
Elphinstone High School, **14**, 72-73
Emerson's fountain, **66**
Emmanuel Mission Church, **68**
High Court, 53
VT, 89
Napier Road, 140
National Bank, 115
National Gallery of Modern Art, 135
neo-Classical style, 10
Army & Navy Store, 112
Chartered Bank, 113, **114**
early 19th century Bombay, 15, 17, 30
National Bank, 115
neo-Gothic style, **11**, **17**
challenged, 98, 99, 102, 112, 126
Convocation Hall, 45
dean of the style, 78, 86, 118
decoration, 20, 38, 43
early experiments, 15
Frere's vision, 37, 120
GPO, 57
High Court, 53, 54
Rajabai Tower, 44
Sailors' Home, 97
St John's Church, 16
university extension, 41
with Tudor style, 117
New Delhi, 128, 135
Nicol Road, 116
Norman style, 132
Nowrojie, Burjorjie, 96
Ohel David Synagogue, 140, 142
Ordish, Rowland Mason, 141
Watson's Hotel, 31-33
Orient Club, 118, 135, 139
Oriental Buildings, **37**
Oval Maidan, 37, 38, 39, 52, 53, **136-137**
P D'Mello (Frere) Road, 106
Palazzo Contarini del Bovolo, **134**
Panwell Brick Kiln & Machine Co, 62
Paris, Walter, 78, 140, 141
Cathedral High School, 72
Elphinstone College, 60
GPO, 56-57, 97
High Court, 52
Telegraph Office, 97
university, 41

Parsis, 18, 30
Perpendicular style, 132
Philip, J Birnie, 140
Phule, Mahatma Jyotiba, 62
Police Court, 75
Police Headquarters, 96
poppoi capitals, 24
Porbandar stone, 18, 30, 38, 41, 44, 48, 50, 57, 59, 64, 65, 70, 71, 90, 106, 107, 113, 116
Pre-Raphaelites, 39, 133
Prichard, John, 138
Progress sculpture, **86**, **87**, 92
Public Works Department. *See* PWD
Pugin, AWN, 11, 15, 18
PWD, 51, 101, 120, 138, 139, 140, 141
amalgamation with Royal Engineers, 28
fees, 23
office building, 54-55, 56
Secretariat, 38
VT, 87
R Kamani Road. *See* Nicol Road
Rajabai Tower (university clock tower), **29**, 40, 41, 43, 44-45, **47**, **132**, **136**
Ramchander, Muccoond, 51
Ramparts Removal Committee, 21, 28, 56, 78, 141
Ransome's Patent Stone, 38, 56
Rashtrapati Bhavan, 126
interior, **125**
Ratnagiri granite, 30, 45
RBYC, 34, 138
Residential Chambers, 117, 138
reading room
University Library, 42-44
David Sassoon Library, 58-59
Readymoney, Sir Cowasjee Jehangier, 18, 40, **48**, 50, 60, 142
Reay, Lord, 92
Renaissance, 135
Italian, 134, 135
Renaissance Revival style, 135
rib vault, 10
RIBA, 29, 69, 100, 129, 138
Romanesque style, 132, 133
rose window
Convocation Hall, 50
Magistrate's Court, 76
VT, 87, **91**
Royal Academy, 65, 69, 86, 133, 139
Royal Alfred Sailors' Home, 78, 96
Royal Architectural Museum, 25
Royal Bombay Yacht Club. *See*

RBYC

Royal Engineers, 28

Royal Institute of British Architects. *See* RIBA

Roychund, Premchand, 40, **44**

Ruskin, John, 15, 134

Sabrina Fountain, 65

Sassoon, David, 58, 72

Sassoon, Sir Albert, 72

Saunders & Co, 70

School of Art, South Kensington, 23-24

Science and Art Department, South Kensington, 29

Science and Art Museum, South Kensington, 21

Scott, George Gilbert, Jr, 142

Scott, Giles Gilbert, 142

Scott, John Oldrid, 142

Scott, Sir George Gilbert, 11, 128, 140, 141-142
    Afghan church drawings, 16, 17, 29
    St Pancras Station, **81-82**, 87, 142
    University Buildings, 40-51, 54, 61, **134**, **136-137**

Scott & McClelland, 58, 115

Scottish Baronial style, 116

Secretariat, 38-39, 40, 55, 138

Seoni sandstone, 51, 90

Shahid Bhagat Singh Marg, 96

Shoorji Vallabhdas Marg. *See* Ballard Road

Shurikersett, J, 93

Sir Jamsetjee Jeejeebhoy Hospital, 15

Sir Jamsetjee Jeejeebhoy School of Art. *See* JJ School of Art

Smirke, Sir Robert, 142

Smith, Thomas Roger, 29, 140, 141
    double roof, 22, 32
    GPO design, 56, 57
    guidelines, 28, 29, 38, 39, 121, 123, 128, 129-130
    suggestions for JJ School, 22, 23

South Kensington style, 135

St Andrew's Kirk, 15

St Giles, Camberwell, 142

St John's Church, Colaba, 16-19
    128, 138, 139
    high altar, **19**

St Pancras Station, London, **81-82**, 87, 142

St Paul's Church, 67, 68, 70

St Thomas's Cathedral, 51

stained glass, 11
    BMC, 104, 105
    Emmanuel Mission Church, 70

St John's, 17, **18**, **19**
    university, **25**, 41, 42, 50, 51

Standard Chartered Bank, **115**

Stevens & Co, 139

Stevens, Charles F, 107, 113, 114, 116, 118, 135, 139

Stevens, Frederick William, 78
    BB&CI commission, 107-111, 128
    birth, 78
    BMC commission, 98, 100-105, 128
    built work, 79-117, 125, 128
    death, 113, 114, 118, 128
    Indo-Saracenic style, 78, 98, 99, 106, 111, 112
    Italian Gothic style, 93
    Italianate neo-Classical style, 113
    Lucknow college design, 78
    partnership with Gostling, 112, 139
    private practice, 101
    Ramparts Removal Committee, 78
    Sailors' Home, 78, 96-97
    Scottish Baronial style, 116
    VT, 76, 79-93, 107, 128

Street, George Edmund, 11, 54, 61, 98

Suez Canal, 25, 79

Taylor roof tiles, 41, 58

Telegraph Office, 78, 97, 140, 141

Telegraph Signallers' Quarters, 78, 141

Terry, GW, 21

Teulon, Samuel Sanders, 11

Times of India, The, 51, 69, 131

thermantidotes, 32

Town Hall, 15, 20

Triggs, BG, 139

Trubner & Co, 98

Trubshawe, James, 28, 140, 141
    departure from Bombay, 56
    Elphinstone College, 60-61
    GPO, 56, 57
    High Court, 52
    plan for Bombay, 150-151
    Ramparts Removal Committee, 28, 56

Tudor style, 117

Tulsi reservoir, 138

University College, London, 29

University Buildings, 40-51, 136

university clock tower. *See* Rajabai Tower

University Library, **29**, 40, 41-44, **46**, **47**, 134

Urbs Prima in Indis, 16, 103

V&A, London, 140

Vanbrugh, Sir John, 135

Vasai stone, 24, 30, 59, 68, 112

Veer Nariman Road. *See* Church Gate Street

Venice, Palazzo Ducale, **43**

Venetian Gothic style, 14, 98, 134
    BB&CI offices, 111
    High Court, **52**, 53, 54
    Magistrate's Court, 76
    PWD office, 55
    Secretariat, 55
    university, 43, **136-137**
    Wilkins, 55, 142

verandas, 29, 34, 48, 97

Victoria & Albert Museum. *See* V&A

Victoria Memorial Hall, Kolkata, 135, 138

Victoria Terminus. *See* VT

Vihar waterworks, 138

VT, 76, 79-95, 96, 98, 99, 103, 104, 107, 128
    1890s' view, **83-84**, **121**
    booking hall, **88**, 89-90
    central dome, 86, 87, 92, 100
    decorative style, 93
    exterior decoration, 90-93, **94-95**, **120**
    gardens, 89
    location, 89
    St Pancras as model, **81-84**, 87
    train sheds, **83**, 89
    watercolour perspective, 79, **80**, **85**, 86

Vuillamy, Lewis, 139

Wailes, William, 17
    stained glass, 17, **18**

Walton, Rienzi Giesman, 66

Watson, John Hudson, 33

Watson's Hotel, 31-34, 112
    annexe, 34, 100

Western Railway. *See* BB&CI

Westminster Abbey, 14

Westwood Bailey & Co, 45

Whitehead, TK, 69

Wilkins, General Henry St Clair, 38-39, 54-55, 140, 142

Willcock, Indo-Saracenic style, **122-123**, **126**

Wilson, John, 71

Wilson College, 71, 138

Wimbridge & Co, 105

Wittet, George, 126, 135
    Edwardian Baroque style, **125**

Wodehouse, Sir Philip, 50

Wood, John, 138

Woolner, Thomas, 58

Wren, Sir Christopher, 135

Wyatt, Matthew Digby, 29

ACKNOWLEDGEMENTS

I would like to thank Colin Cunningham, Vikas Dilawari,
Amol Divkar, Kimball Higgs, David Hutchinson,
Sophie Gordon, Homi Kaka, Pradip & Soniya Lalla,
George Michell, Foy Nissen, Bharath Ramamrutham,
and Kenneth Topp. They all helped me in various ways
during the preparation of this book.

ISBN 81-7508-329-8

TEXT

© 2002 Christopher W London

PUBLISHED BY

India Book House Pvt Ltd
Mahalaxmi Chambers, 5th Floor,
22 Bhulabhai Desai Road,
Mumbai 400 026, India
Tel 91 22 2495 3827 Fax 91 22 2493 8406
E-mail info@ibhpublishing.com